Reggie Kray was one of London's most notorious gangsters in the 1950s and '60s. Involved in everything from protection rackets to murder, he was eventually jailed in 1969, and remained in prison until his death in 2000.

Peter Gerrard met Reggie in 1989 and worked on the book with him for the next five years.

Reggie Kray's East End Stories

The Lost Memoirs of the Gangland Legend

REGGIE KRAY
WITH
PETER GERRARD

sphere

SPHERE

First published in Great Britain in 2010 by Sphere
This paperback edition published in 2011 by Sphere
Reprinted 2012 (three times)

Copyright © Reggie Kray and Peter Gerrard
Maps and family tree © John Gilkes

A CIP catalogue record for this book
is available from the British Library.

ISBN 978-0-7515-4710-8

Typeset in Garamond by M Rules
Printed and bound in Great Britain by
Clays Ltd, St Ives plc

Papers used by Sphere are from well-managed forests
and other responsible sources.

MIX
Paper from
responsible sources
FSC® C104740

Sphere
An imprint of
Little, Brown Book Group
100 Victoria Embankment
London EC4Y 0DY

An Hachette UK Company
www.hachette.co.uk

www.littlebrown.co.uk

Contents

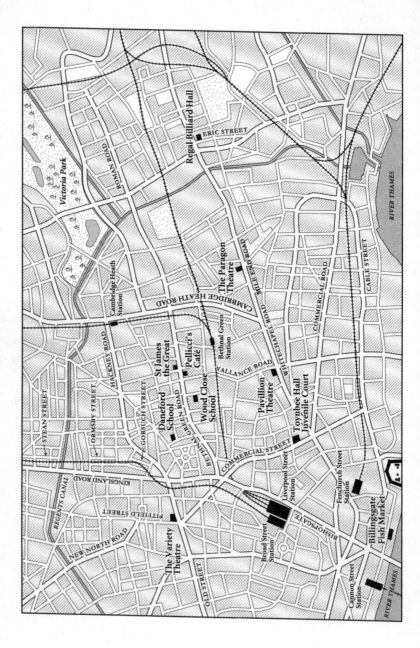

Kray Family Tree

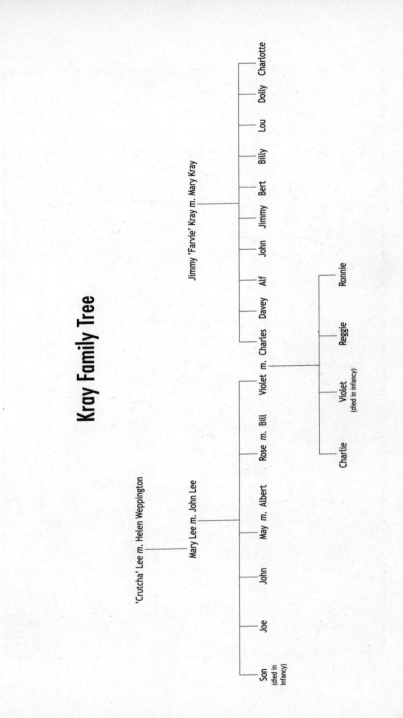

'Crutcha' Lee m. Helen Weppington

Mary Lee m. John Lee

Joe | John | May m. Albert | Rose m. Bill | Violet m. Charles | Son (died in infancy)

Jimmy 'Farvie' Kray m. Mary Kray

Charles | Davey | Alf | John | Jimmy | Bert | Billy | Lou | Dolly | Charlotte

Charlie | Violet (died in infancy) | Reggie | Ronnie

Foreword

Roberta Kray

I first made Reg Kray's acquaintance on a cold March day in 1996. That we ever met at all was purely down to chance. A friend of mine who'd promised to help out with the publicity for a video being made about Reg's late brother Ron, found himself with work commitments abroad and needed someone to take his place. Would I be interested?

During my long nervous wait in the visiting room at HMP Maidstone, being carefully scrutinised by a number of stern-looking prison officers, I had plenty of time to question the wisdom of ever having agreed to the proposition. I wondered what on earth I was doing there and what kind of a man I was about to encounter. I knew very little about the Krays, the only clues I did possess coming courtesy of a seemingly endless string of parodies that had appeared on TV in the 1980s. If these were to be believed, then Reginald Kray could well turn out to be a rather stupid strutting gangster, a man overly keen both to impress and intimidate. How wrong could I be?

As Reg emerged from the door at the back of the hall and quickly walked over to introduce himself, I found myself in the presence of a polite, grey-haired, softly spoken man. It would be wrong to claim that all my reservations instantly disappeared but they were, for the next couple of hours, put on hold. It was his energy and spirit that had the most profound effect on me. Reg Kray, against all the odds, proved himself to be a man of intelligence, determination and humour.

We were very different people, from completely different backgrounds, but through the following months our friendship gradually grew stronger. Prison isn't the easiest of places in which to openly express your emotions – any sign of weakness will be instantly exploited – and I quickly became aware that he found it easier to talk to someone who was outside the system. It is always flattering to be taken into someone's confidence but over the following months it became clear that the bond between us was turning into something deeper.

Through our long conversations I realised that Reg was trying to deal with a number of difficult emotions: grief at the loss of his twin brother; an intense desire to make the most of the present; and a growing frustration at his own uncertain future. It was at difficult periods like these that he looked most often to the past.

Reg had many regrets about his life. He was aware that he had made disastrous decisions, taken wrong roads and done too much damage through the choices he had made. However, there was one thing he always remained proud of and that was his roots in the East End of London. It was to these streets, and the characters which had once peopled them, that – in his mind at least – he could always return. It was these memories that gave him solace and helped him through the darkest hours.

This book is Reg's very personal journey through the place he held most dear. It is a story he started writing many years ago, but to do justice to the people he had known, the people who had shaped him, seemed an almost impossible task. However, he always wanted it to be read. It is now ten years since his death, a fitting time perhaps to reveal a little more about the man behind the public image. Within the pages of this book can be found clues as to what motivated Reg and his twin brother and why they grew up to become two of Britain's most infamous villains. The East End of their childhood, with its tight-knit community and strong, often eccentric characters, was to have an enduring influence.

Reg's grandparents, all of them born around the 1870s, lived in an East End renowned for its poverty and squalor. Vastly over-populated, lawless and disease-ridden, this part of the capital was notorious, and by the 1880s had become known as a place of darkness, of terrible violence, depravity and horror. For the rest of London, this vision was confirmed by the brutal killing spree of Jack the Ripper in 1888. To survive in such an environment took guts, determination and a modicum of luck.

Both of Reg's male grandparents, Jimmy Kray and John 'Cannonball' Lee, were powerful, fighting men. Whether in the boxing ring or on the street, this ability served two useful purposes: they were able to supplement their meagre incomes and could also gain the respect of others. To make a name for yourself – by whatever means – meant that you stood out from the crowd. In the heaving amorphous mass of the East End, this was no small achievement, and this legacy, this burning determination to be *someone*, was duly passed on to their grandsons.

It was the deep-rooted desire not just for fortune but also for fame that undoubtedly contributed to the downfall of the Krays. While other criminals would sensibly keep their heads down, never drawing unwanted attention to themselves, the twins were the very opposite. Being successful was not enough – they needed to be seen to be successful. As such, they frequently courted publicity, mixing with movie stars, politicians and sportsmen, and even going to the extreme of engaging a biographer to write their life story shortly before their arrest. However, while Reg was growing up in the 1930s, all this was a barely imaginable future. Times were tough and with few opportunities to escape from the grinding poverty many young boys like him looked to the famous local boxers, the street fighters and the prosperous villains as examples of how to succeed. Even at a tender age, it must have been clear to Reg that crime *could* pay. To make a good living, you either had to be smart or you had to be tough. But better if you could be both.

Reg was very aware of the hardships his close relatives had endured. They were part of an East End population that felt itself abandoned by the government and, as such, owed little in return. Reg's father, Charles Kray, found himself on the wrong side of the law when he deserted the army, reluctant to 'serve' a country that had shown an utter disregard for the welfare of his grandparents, his parents or his own wife and kids.

Of course it was not just the men of the East End who had a lasting influence on Reg, but the women too. If there was one thing that could always make him smile, it was reminiscing about his mother. One of three feisty sisters, Violet Kray understood what it took to survive and fought a constant battle to keep her children safe and healthy. With her husband often absent, it was left to her to raise her sons and often provide for them too. Reg once told me that one of his most enduring memories was of his mother pawning her wedding ring to put food on the table. Such sacrifices had a profound effect on him.

Although his childhood was a relatively happy one, the future man was inevitably shaped by the attitudes and opinions of his family and the community he lived in. Violence was commonplace in the East End, the easiest solution to any disagreement, and he grew up witnessing many of these battles. When Reg and Ron were older, they tried first to emulate their boxing heroes and had some success in the ring. It soon became clear, however, that there were faster and more lucrative ways to make a living. In *Reggie Kray's East End Stories*, Reg describes their move into the criminal world and the villains they came to know. Some of the names are familiar, others less so, but at the time they were all forces to be reckoned with.

The downfall of the Kray twins has been well documented but the reasons for how and why they originally rose to power have been vague. Some answers, I believe, lie within the pages of this book.

Finally, it is necessary to say that just as the past could bring Reg comfort, it could bring him great pain too. Nostalgia is all well and good, but sometimes the knowledge of everything that has been lost – and why it has been lost – is almost too much to bear. He had been raised with the idea that to be someone was everything; of the importance of standing out at any cost – but the price he paid turned out to be a great one. At his death in October 2000, he had already served over thirty-two years in prison. If the various legacies of the East End were what made Reg Kray, then perhaps, in the final reckoning, they were partly what destroyed him too.

Introduction

Peter Gerrard

In 1993 while researching a friend of Reg Kray's – gun for hire, Alfie Gerard – I wrote to Reg with a request for information. I knew that he received in excess of fifty to sixty letters a day, so had little expectation of getting a reply. Imagine my surprise when I got a letter from him asking for my telephone number.

Replying to letters can be an expensive exercise for prisoners on their low wages, so a way round this was to reuse the stamps. The stamp would be coated with colourless PVA glue and left to dry. Once received all the recipient had to do was wipe off any franking mark with a damp cloth, and hey presto a clean stamp. 'Save the trees' written on the envelope alerted the prisoner as to what to expect.

Days after I'd sent him my telephone number, Reggie called me at eight o'clock one morning, introducing himself with, 'Reggie Kray here.' He had a very distinct voice, soft and slightly high-pitched. We talked for ten minutes or so and finished with him inviting me to visit him at Blundeston Prison with a small bottle of brandy in a plastic bottle to avoid detection, a service I provided for many years.

Driving into the picturesque village of Blundeston, I felt a certain level of trepidation as I had no idea what sort of man I would shortly be meeting. Once inside the prison I was uncomfortably aware of the brandy bottle I had hidden inside my waistband. I sat in the bright visitor's hall and waited as the prisoners filed in. Any fears I might have had disappeared as soon as Reggie appeared and gave me a friendly hug. He was shorter in height than I expected, but I couldn't help noticing his toned physique. What struck me most was the size of his hands – definitely fighter's hands, and it wasn't too long before one of them grazed my chin as he demonstrated his infamous cigarette punch. Back in 1994 smoking was still allowed in the prison and taking a cigarette from a packet on the table Reggie offered it directly to my mouth. One's instinct is to take the proffered cigarette with an open mouth and this is when he strikes, with the open mouth guaranteeing a broken jaw – fortunately he was only demonstrating this time.

We were constantly interrupted by well-wishers approaching the table to shake Reggie's hand or give him a hug and every one of them was received with the same patient and friendly demeanour. Autographs were sought or thanks were given for looking after a certain prisoner. It was obvious that Reggie had a great deal of respect from all and for all. Over the years I have spoken to many celebrities and too many are so full of themselves they bring the shutters down when the conversation veers away from them and theirs. Not with Reggie. He showed great interest in my working life and particularly my family.

All the while we spoke he sipped at an orange drink bought from the canteen, to which he added the contraband brandy. By the end of our two-hour visit his face was visibly red and I felt sure he would be pulled up on the way back to his cell, but that never seemed to happen. It was obvious he was fascinated by his family's past. He spoke at great length about where his family had come from and little about the crimes that had seen him locked away for so long.

After a few visits, Reggie was moved to Maidstone Prison. This was a much more forbidding place – castle-like, it dominated the lower part of the town. Again I ran the gauntlet of suspicious screws when, as usual, I smuggled in illicit brandy. All visitors for Ronnie and Reggie are searched upon entering the prison. One had a choice: refuse the search and be asked to leave, or front it out – I chose the latter, hoping that the pat-down would not be too intimate. I managed to get through, but was sweating profusely by the time I did. A young girl accompanying me was not so fortunate. Reggie had asked me to bring her in on my visiting order and having had the usual request, she was happily carrying a bottle of brandy in her handbag – the first thing the screws search. Out came the bottle and was held up high for all to see. The chief screw reacted angrily, threatening her with arrest. Perhaps softened by her tears he confiscated the drink and warned her he would not be so accommodating should it happen again. I was directly behind her and the screw apologised to me for the upset, little knowing that I too was carrying a bottle of brandy.

Once inside and Reggie was sitting opposite me, he immediately introduced me to many of his convict friends and we made quite a party of it, with the booze flowing freely. As his way of showing appreciation for any visit, Reggie always liked to give some small gift, which, with little to give, invariably took the form of a crayon or pencil drawing. He was eager for news of the outside world and of the word on mutual friends.

A month or so after we first met, Reggie asked me if I'd be interested in working with him on a book. The many conversations we'd had concerning his family had inspired him to make a record of them. Much could be collected during our two-hour visits, while more could be written by Reggie in the privacy of his cell. So he set to work.

Once I had established myself as someone trustworthy, Reggie asked me to visit his brother Ronnie in Broadmoor hospital, perhaps to gain a second opinion of my character.

I had the same feeling of trepidation as I was led through the gardens of Broadmoor towards Ronnie's block. But as before this feeling dissipated immediately upon meeting him. We had a visit in a private room and after pulling my chair out for me Ron politely asked if he could get me a coffee, which he went off to fetch. I found talking to Ron like talking to a friendly uncle. The only time he showed a spark of anger was when I mentioned I had bumped into Peter Sutcliffe, the Yorkshire Ripper, on the way in. He said, 'I fucking hate that man for doing things to women like he did, but he'll get what's coming to him.' And true enough, much later he arranged for someone to stab Sutcliffe in the eye, blinding him. We mainly discussed the world in general and Ron's plans for the future when, hopefully, he would be released. He confessed he was tired of being locked away and wanted nothing more from life than to travel and then settle down in the countryside.

From what one reads the impression given is that Ronnie was the dominant twin and that Reggie followed. Whether this had once been the case I don't know, but now Ronnie did what Reggie said. He asked me to write a piece for the newspapers putting forward his side of his relationship with his ex-wife Kate Kray. I agreed and took down the story. But Reggie vetoed the idea a few days later with no explanation. This kind of thing happened on more than one occasion.

In conversation one day, I admired a heavy gold ring on

Ronnie's little finger. He told me it was a gift from an American Mafia godfather, then without hesitation took it off and offered it to me. I had to refuse his generous offer, much as I would have liked to accept it. It gave me a good insight into his character. In the few years he had left, I paid many visits to Broadmoor and enjoyed each one immensely.

Sadly Ronnie died in 1995 and Reggie invited me to his funeral. Three cars behind the hearse, sitting with the late Lenny Mclean and the late Tony Lambrianou, I was amazed at the spectacle of our journey to the church. The streets were packed with spectators, and policemen saluted at every junction. Nothing like it had been seen since the funeral of Winston Churchill. Once inside the equally packed church I could see Reggie in the front row looking very sad. I weaved my way through the crowd and approached him. A big smile lit up his face and he jumped to his feet to give me a hug, almost dragging the screw he was handcuffed to off the pew. It was a sad day and as we left the church to the strains of 'I Will Always Love You', villains or not there was hardly a dry eye among the congregation.

I was also invited to meet their elder brother Charlie in Croydon, where he was based. Although completely different from the twins, I found him to be charming, humorous, extremely friendly and the best of company. I was amazed when he was sentenced to twelve years at the age of seventy for some dubious involvement in a drugs deal. He only served three years before dying in 2000, six months before his brother, Reggie.

Looking at Reggie and listening to him over the years of visiting I was struck by what a very strong man he was to have suffered so long behind bars but still be able to remain with it and positive – I don't ever recall hearing him complain about his situation. Perhaps his past was not admirable but I could not help admiring his strength of character. Though he looked forward to his forthcoming parole hearing he seemed to have accepted his lot and bore it with patience and fortitude – a clue as to how he rose so high in his chosen profession in the underworld.

1

Back Home

Over the last twenty-six years I can't think of any one time when I have been able to relax, lie back and listen to utter silence. Because even when a prison is quiet it's still noisy by the rest of the world's standards. I think back to when we lived in a rambling old mansion we owned deep in the Surrey countryside. There, set in nine acres of gardens and paddocks, I often found moments when everything stood still. This could happen at any time of the day, any time of the year, and then I could close my eyes and there would be nothing. No birdsong, no cars, no rustle of wind in the trees, not even the distant barking of a dog, and I would feel my cares and problems wash away from me. Deprived of that small pleasure I am often very conscious

---

of how much I miss the solitude that profound silence can bring.

It doesn't matter where you go in the prison system, there is always that hum of an institution. During the day there is a constant buzz of noise: shouting, laughing, singing, crashing of doors, radios blaring, the never-ending sound of footsteps; and in the dead of night a muffled cough or cries of distress are there to break into one's reverie. Still, with the single cells we are allocated here at Maidstone, the hours between 7.45 p.m. and 7.45 a.m. can at least be spent in much-needed privacy. Though I enjoy my days spent among friends, I find that as the day wears on I am looking forward to bang-up, in perhaps a similar way a working man looks forward to going home, putting his feet up and relaxing.

To the screws, the secure rooms they lock us into overnight are cells, nothing more, nothing less. But to the individual prisoner it is his home and in fact I refer to mine as my flat. Each time a cell is vacated due to the transfer or release of the previous occupant, it is stripped out, searched thoroughly and left in a basic state for the next con. The authorities supply a minimum of comfort and it's up to the individual to put his own mark on the place. When I arrived here early in 1994 from Blundeston Prison in Suffolk, the furnishings consisted of a bed, a chair, a table, and a couple of cupboards. Hardly the most welcoming sight when you know that you will be spending twelve hours of every day locked up inside it for the next ten years. But in no time at all I had transformed this bleak room into a cosy study with the help of friends and supporters outside who supplied me with what was needed; a soft carpet and lemon-coloured curtains with pelmets and matching bedspread soon put a bit of warmth into the room. I added a comfortable settee, another table, an aquarium holding nine fish, and my music system. Here and there I placed treasured ornaments and mementos and hung photographs of family and friends on the walls. Now it was truly home.

You may know that I was being held in Lewes Prison, Sussex, in the early nineties. From there I was shipped out to HMP Blundeston, which is situated on the edge of the Dickensian village of the same name, not many miles from Lowestoft. What I would have given to have wandered freely along the wooded lanes and narrow streets of the village, but all I could do was gaze in frustration through secure windows at the tantalising view of red pantiled rooftops and church spire. Having read and enjoyed many books by Charles Dickens I would love to have walked around and physically touched the local landmarks he mentioned so often in *David Copperfield*: the church, the Plough Inn, and the white-walled thatched cottage, named The Rookery, which was the home of the book's hero. While I never visited this village when I was a free man, I was no stranger to Suffolk, as it was not far from here that Ron and I had owned and lived, for a time, in a mansion, known as The Brooks. We all loved it there, including our parents who lived in the gatehouse on and off for a long time. We were both saddened to see it sold off after our arrest.

I had no complaint against Blundeston Prison other than it was a great distance for my friends and family to travel for visits. Today the prison authorities try and place inmates within a reasonable distance of their home town or where their families live. Though, with a touch of cynicism, I feel this is more to do with economics than compassion. When a husband or father is imprisoned, in many cases his family is forced to rely on government hand-outs to survive, which then makes them eligible for visiting expenses if they have to travel over a certain distance. Logical then to move the con and save some money. I wish this system had been in place when my mother was alive. It broke my heart when I thought of the toll it must have taken on her to visit her sons, particularly in her later years. Not that she ever complained – that wasn't in her nature – but imagine the strain of getting from the East End to Parkhurst on the Isle of Wight, or Gartree way up north.

Most of my family and close friends made the effort to visit me in Blundeston but many more, much as they would have liked to, could not and I understood. So with this in mind it was not too long before I applied for a transfer to Maidstone. More than two years were to pass before my request was granted and even then it was unclear as to when

I would get my actual moving date. First I was told it would be the end of this week, and then it was changed to the week after that. A month would pass and another date would be given only for me to see it pass once more. By the time it became definite I was completely pissed off and only really cheered up when I was actually on the prison coach.

I can tell you I gave a loud sigh of relief when the coach pulled away from the prison gates. An hour passed and just as I was thinking that at this rate we will be there in no time, a call came through on the mobile telephone. One of the screws said something to the driver and he immediately pulled over into a lay-by and stopped. The other prisoners and I sat quietly and watched the staff climb from the coach and go into a huddle of gesticulating arms and raised voices. A thought passed through my head: Here we go. They've realised their mistake and I shouldn't be on the coach. I held my breath until a screw climbed back on board and told us that all our medical papers had been left behind, so we would have to wait until a taxi brought them from the prison.

We sat in that lay-by for two hours. At first it made a pleasant change to sit and study a fresh view of rolling fields, trees and cloud formations, but in my highly charged state of anticipation at seeing old friends at Maidstone, I soon became impatient and lost interest. Eventually the documents were brought from the prison by private taxi and we were on our way at last.

Twenty minutes later, the coach began to shudder and once again the driver pulled over, this time in a cloud of steam. I just leant back and closed my eyes – this was not my day. The coach was beyond repair, at least at the roadside, so again we would have to wait. To save us hanging about for hours I suggested to one of the screws that he should phone for a police van and get us taken to a local prison where we could be picked up later. Much to my surprise he took my advice. A van turned up soon after and we were taken to Felsham Prison for tea and a meal. By the time we had finished, a coach had been made available and was ready and waiting to take us to our destination.

As we crossed the new road bridge at Dartford, perhaps two hundred feet above the Thames, I looked out of the window and gazed up the long stretch of darkened river. Somewhere, beyond the million sparkling lights, unseen yet only a dozen miles away, lay the East End, and at that moment I felt closer to home than I had done for more years than I can remember. A memory popped into my head of sitting in Pellicci's Café on the Bethnal Green Road savouring a coffee and talking to good friends. Does the café, which has been there since the turn of the century, still open its doors every day? Does pencil-moustached Nevio Pellicci still bustle around shouting orders through to his wife Maria, or Mama as she was known? That place served the best food outside of your own mother's kitchen and it still makes my mouth water at the thought.

The rolling, wooded countryside of Kent brought back a memory of when I had driven through these same parts well over forty years before. Ron, myself and two friends stole a car from the Roman Road area. I can't remember what make of car it was but I can still recall the smell of rich leather upholstery and the excitement we felt as we sped through the Blackwall Tunnel and out into the country. I think we got as far as a place named Shorne before we ran off the road and wrecked the front of the car on a stone road sign. Thinking it a great joke, we shoved it into a field beside a haystack, pulled some sheaves over it, and then thumbed a lift back to London on the back of a lorry.

Hoping time would pass quickly, I closed my eyes and once again let my mind drift back into the past. Twenty-six years in captivity: I can hardly believe that passage of time. With a sentence of thirty years there is little point in scratching off each day on a calendar. I'm reminded of Henri Charrière who wrote *Papillon*. He was imprisoned on Devil's Island and spent many years in solitary confinement. When given a sentence of, say, four years he would say to himself, 'That's only eight periods of six months', and would scratch off each six as they passed. I still think our sentence was too harsh but, like it or not, there was nothing else to do but knuckle down and see it out. As any con knows, the first years were the worst and I have to admit I kicked against the system. If a screw looked at me the wrong way I'd knock him on his back. These people whom I would never tolerate for a moment outside the prison had my every hour in their control. 'Do this, do that' was never something that I was good at accepting. Eventually I realised no matter what I did, the system was always going to be bigger than me and I settled down to do my time. So, I suppose, they won in the end. I eventually decided that the only way to accept incarceration without going mad was to acknowledge that these walls were my home for however long it would take. Forget the outside. Don't torture yourself with what could have been.

A misconception that many people have is that because of my notoriety I get some sort of special treatment inside. This couldn't be further from the truth: this is not America, where the John Gottis can buy themselves luxury. I am treated the same as the lowliest con. The only difference might be that I find I am fortunate enough to get a lot of respect from those around me. I spent many years on Category A, which is like being in a prison inside a prison. You're watched constantly and visitors are rigorously investigated by the police before they are allowed to visit. This in itself prevented many of my friends from coming to see me because of their criminal records. At the same time, a number of my friends were themselves in the system, so I was not without company by any means.

My weekly wage is in the region of six pounds and from this one is expected to buy all the necessities for daily life and if there is any left over to buy little luxuries like the odd chocolate bar. No, Ronnie and myself are not living the high life on squirrelled-away millions; all our money soon disappeared as the years passed and, sad to say, we have to get by on the munificence of others. I must say I am blessed in having legions of followers on the outside who send in money, trainers, stamps and other materials.

With so many years behind me, I am now looking forward to my next parole hearing. I am quietly confident that I will get the result I am hoping for. After all, I have kept my nose clean for years now and glide along in the system from day to day bringing no disruption to the daily life of the prison. In fact, I think I do a certain amount of good as my reputation means I am listened to when I give sound advice to young tearaways. I only have to point at my own tariff for them to see that crime does not pay. It might seem to in the short term, but eventually the law will catch up with you and then you have to pay the price. There is nothing macho about spending years behind the door, away from friends and family with your life on hold.

One of my greatest sorrows was being separated from my brother Ronnie when we were sentenced. I am very rarely allowed to visit him in Broadmoor, and when I am able I am handcuffed, shackled and stuck inside a van with four screws for the trip to Berkshire, which takes a couple of hours and can be most unpleasant in the heat of summer. What do they think I am going to do at my age? Overpower the screws and make a bid for freedom? Perhaps many years ago one might have thought of some means of escape but with my freedom on the horizon I'm not likely to attempt to escape now.

The view out of the steamy window, stretching down the hill and towards the centre of Maidstone and the prison, snapped me out of my reminiscing. We had arrived. Hours late, but at last I was here. Once I was passed through reception, the frustrations of the day were soon forgotten as I met two of my closest friends, Joe Martin and John Heibner, in an emotional reunion. I had not set eyes on either of these men for almost fifteen years. I first met Joe back in 1964 when Ron and I were in the Green Dragon Social Club, down Aldgate. We were introduced, had a drink together and, as often happens when you meet a sound person, we hit it off immediately. Sadly, the time we were to spend together in the free world outside was limited. A couple of years after our first meeting, Joe was convicted of murder while carrying out a robbery armed with a shotgun. This man who fought with honour and bravery for his country during the Korean War was given a savage sentence and today, twenty-nine years later, he is still paying the price for that one mistake. The taking of a life is not to be taken lightly, it's a very serious mistake, but what can be achieved by keeping him locked up year after year with little hope of release? I know he has always regretted what he did, so surely this remorse must count for something. At sixty-one years of age he will never reoffend, so I think he should be allowed to spend his remaining years as a free man in peace and happiness.

Some years after Joe was sent away, Ron and me were destined to follow him. Ron spent a number of years with him in Durham Prison, while I got to know him even better when we served time together in the top security block at Parkhurst. I am proud to state that I love him like a brother and with few in the system like him he has my greatest respect.

John Heibner is roughly ten years younger than me and I've known him since he was a teenager. He spent a lot of time in our company and I'll always remember the time Ron, myself and some of the firm went along to Repton Boxing Club to watch him in action against John H. Stacey. It was only a friendly spar that Ron had arranged, but we were pleased to see our young friend put up a good show against the man who in later years was to become Welterweight Champion of the World. John was a useful and loyal member of the firm right up until we were arrested on the Cornell and McVitie murders. After that, the next time I was to meet him was when he was brought into the hospital block inside Parkhurst Prison after an assault on a screw. This is normal procedure after a prisoner has had a flare-up and did not mean he had been hurt in any way. I was pleased to see him again but shocked when he told me he had recently been given a life sentence with a recommendation of twenty-five years. This was for the alleged contract killing of Beatrice

Gold who owned a dress factory in Clerkenwell. She had been shot in the head. John swore to me that he was innocent and over the twenty years he has served since he has never wavered in this plea. My mother Violet was a very good judge of character and I know she thought the world of him. After we went away and up until it was his turn, he kept an eye open for her to make sure she was all right and for that I'll always be grateful to him.

Apart from meeting old and trusted friends once more, the move to Maidstone allowed me to receive visits on a more regular basis from many other people from the outside. In no time at all, my visiting days were a social event to be looked forward to. In a way it was these visits by old friends that prompted me to write down further reminiscences of my life as our conversations sparked off my memories.

Now that I am more accessible I find that I am seeing people that for various reasons I have not seen for many, many years and, almost without exception, our conversations follow a similar pattern. After the initial greeting and catching up on news, around the time of our third cup of tea from the canteen, my visitor will say, 'Do you remember?' and off we'll go on a pleasant trip down memory lane. 'Do you remember that time we had a sort-out with the Pachita mob?' Or 'What about that time your granddad squared up to that fella in the pub?' 'Bet you don't remember the time you fell in the canal.' And, yes, I did remember them as though they were yesterday.

Banged up at night, I'd run the day through my mind — something I've done all my life — those revived memories would conjure up others. Faces and incidents blurred in my subconscious would spring out with fresh clarity and I'd find myself laughing out loud or at other times wiping a tear from my eyes.

I never cease to be amazed by the infinite capacity of the brain. It seems that nothing we have ever seen or heard is lost or forgotten. It just needs a word, a tune or an evocative scent and immediately the brain releases what we might have thought were forgotten images into the conscious mind.

I find that I have total recall. Why, I don't know. It may be a gift or more likely a practised art. My habit of running the day and all its incidents through my mind as I settle down to sleep I am sure fixes thoughts into my mind for ever. In many ways this can be a double-edged sword, for while memories are all I have left of many people and places, some things are best left buried deep and forgotten.

It was quite a coincidence that, having decided to keep myself busy by noting down memories, I should get a letter urging me to write a book. That same evening I approached bang-up with the sense of excitement that always fills me when I am embarking on a new project. Strangely enough, the thought of deliberately evoking the past gave me a feeling of anticipation, as alone in my room I would once more be seeing in my mind people and places from the past.

Armed with a large flask of boiling water, so that I could make tea at any hour, I made my way up to my flat in readiness for lock-up at quarter to eight. To those of you outside who at this time of night are getting ready to go down to the pub or club, this must seem ridiculously early for grown men to be shut in for the night. But this is the way of the system and over the years I have got used to and accept such routine without complaint.

Over the years I have taken a great interest in the customs and life-style of American Indians. I find that their philosophies are very similar to my own: respect, a code of honour and the ability to face adversity without complaint. I read everything I can about these proud people. Pawnee, Cheyenne, Sitting Bull, Cochise, Red Cloud – magical names that transport me back to our Saturday morning cinema where we would shout ourselves hoarse as the cavalry came over the hill to wipe out the 'damned Redskin'.

One of the less spiritual habits I have copied from the American Indian is that of sleeping on the ground, which they felt brought them closer to the spirits of nature. In my case, with the bare earth beyond my reach, I accept second best and stretch out on the concrete floor. With a sheepskin blanket under me and a similar one over me for warmth, I rest my head on a hard pillow and by ten past eight I am asleep. Five hours later I awake totally refreshed and eager for the new day. It is now as quiet as it can ever be in a prison. Not silent, but quiet enough for thought and contemplation.

Later in the day I will have a strenuous work-out in the gym, but for now fifty press-ups tone me up and get the blood going. I follow this with a cold wash at the basin. Then from the flask make the first of many cups of strong tea that I will drink during the day, and pen in hand I'm ready to lose myself in memories of the past.

2

Forefathers

For you to understand the person I am you will have to be aware not only of the environment I came from and the people I grew up with, but my life in the context of the morality and hardships of those times. You also have to look further back to the lives and living conditions of those that came before me, because it was their conditions and standards that would eventually shape mine.

The East End has always been a world apart from the rest of London. Up until the late 1940s it was notorious for its slums, poverty, disease, prostitution and villainy. I'm no historian so I cannot say why this area should have been singled out to be a place akin to a hell on earth, but from what I have read on the subject during the period in which my grandparents were born, which for all of them was roughly in the 1870s, almost one million people were crammed into an area of less than two or three square miles. When you think that Queen Victoria was well into her reign at this time, the medieval descriptions of the east of the city are almost unbelievable.

In earlier times, villages such as Hoxton, Haggerston and the cottages built around the Bethnal Green must have been almost rural as they were near the River Thames and just outside the bustling city. But as the population grew steadily and more housing was necessary each little village or hamlet was swallowed up until they became one. The beginning of the nineteenth century saw an even greater influx of families seeking work and their fortunes on the fabled 'streets paved with gold'. What might once have been reasonably designed housing was now to become a haphazard jigsaw as three-storey tenements were squeezed into every possible space, with access through dismal courts and dark alleyways.

I suppose that for a time the housing was used as intended – perhaps a family per floor and conditions were not too bad. But then as general unrest and economic problems swept through Europe, with the potential famine in Ireland and lowering standards in our own agricultural system, the tide of immigration to the rich city became a torrent. On finding that London was not the Utopia they expected and with little work to be had, the migrants gradually gravitated downwards until they collected in the sump that was the East End. Within this hopeless ghetto there were three classes: the poor who had a regular job and brought in around a pound a week; the very poor who might manage to scrape together half this amount; and at the bottom a nameless group who barely subsisted on Church charity and scraps. These people lived hand to mouth, not weekly but hour to hour.

This would have been the sort of society my grandparents set up home in. I don't know at what level they lived in their earlier days, but whether poor or penniless, the conditions they would have had to put up with were the same for everyone. The only difference money could make was how often and how well they ate, whether they had warm clothes and footwear, or whether their kids lived or died.

The same tenements that at one time housed three families would be let to any family who could find the rent money. Each room not much bigger than twice the size of my current cell, would probably be home to mother, father and anything up to ten children at a rent of roughly three or four shillings a week, which could be more than half their income. For this the tenant could expect a cold damp room crawling with well-established vermin and fleas. A toilet in the yard would serve all of the possible one hundred tenants. If they were fortunate they would have a single cold water tap on each floor; if not, all water for drinking and washing would have to be fetched from a standpipe in the yard. These water supplies would often be the cause of cholera outbreaks due to cesspits and overflowing drains contaminating the supply.

While a good mother might do her best to keep the family's room clean, it's understandable that with enough problems on her plate she wouldn't have the inclination to touch anything outside her own front door. So it's not hard to imagine the state of the stairs leading up to the rooms, stinking from the caked mud and worse that puddled in the yard. With the authorities turning a blind eye to this no-go area of the East End, the cobbles must have been swimming in rotting garbage and sewage that leaked endlessly from broken and unrepaired drains. What had changed since medieval times? The smell wouldn't have been any different from those days when the better classes held a small posy of flowers under their noses to ward off the stench.

It's in this indescribable place that my grandparents arrived to find work and raise their families. I like to think they were at the top end of that society, and knowing that our family has a trait for always fighting against adversity, I am sure they were. The fact that they raised families at all must mean something in a time when over half the children born in the East End never saw their fifth birthday.

On my mother's side, my great-grandparents were a mixture of nationalities. My Nanny Lee's father was a heavily built blue-eyed, fair-haired German. In later years if mention of him was made in conversation Nan would add in a conspiratorial whisper, 'Not one of the bad ones though.' Her mother, fiercely Irish, was in appearance the opposite of her husband – dark-eyed, dark-haired and dark-complexioned, and her temper could match her looks too. An incident happened when Nan was a young girl that gave her mother a reputation for viciousness. Nan was cutting bread for a meal and either day-dreaming or hungry she cut more than was necessary. Ignoring a cry that the bread had to last until the following day, she continued cutting. Her mother jumped up, grabbed the knife out of her hand and stuck it in her daughter's wrist shouting, 'Now stop when I tell you.' She bore a scar and a painful wrist for the rest of her life. Even in her nineties she wore a band around it to ease the pain of arthritis. In fairness to my great-grandmother perhaps it wasn't an evil temper that drove her to act in that way. She may have been, like many mothers in those days, driven to near breaking-point, worrying about where the next half-penny was coming from.

At that time the Lee family lived just off Brick Lane and one night when she was about ten years of age Nan was woken up by the lamplighter's voice in the street outside, calling, 'Don't go out. Ripper's been about.' She told me that she pulled the blankets over her head, cowering in fear. The following day they discovered that one of Jack the Ripper's victims, Annie Chapman, had been found under the arches in Hanbury Street just around the corner from where they lived.

Nanny Lee could remember a time, when she was even

younger, of passing a shop opposite the London Hospital where the Elephant Man was on display, at an entrance fee of twopence. It was out of the question that her mother would waste so much money on frivolity, so she never did see him. In later years she would look at the exploitation of unfortunate people as wrong but she would say that in those days it was all quite normal.

I don't know anything of Grandad Lee's mother apart from her name, which was Helen Weppington and she was known to her grandchildren as Nanny Wepp. His father was a gypsy cattle drover and had a name I've never heard anywhere else, Crutcha – which may have been a nickname but he was never known as anything else. Originally he could have settled in any part of the country but because of his work, bringing cattle and sheep into London, he would regularly have found himself on the main drove into the city – which was Whitechapel Road. That is why it is one of the widest roads to be found in the city. Part of his job would have been to slaughter the cattle or sheep he had driven, so when tiring of the hardships of the road where else would he have looked to find settled work than the abattoirs of the East End. For a man with ambition, natural progression from the slaughterhouse would have been to become a butcher himself. And this he did, eventually setting up the first butcher's shop in Smithfield Market. Being out of sight or sound of the market for so long I cannot be sure that it is still in place, but on a wall in the market, there used to be a plaque bearing the words 'Lee and Cody', commemorating the fact that they were founders of the market. Who Cody was I've no idea as I never heard that Crutcha Lee had a partner.

Unfortunately for a man who had pulled himself up from nothing, he was to end the last seventeen years of his life confined to a mental hospital or an epilepsy institution, which was probably one and the same thing at the time. No one knew what brought on his epilepsy but there was an occasion when he had an accident while driving one of his double-horse carts. It was a winter's night and it had been raining. As it got dark the weather turned icy. Standing up to draw the horses to rein he slipped on the iced-over footboard and fell between the shafts, receiving a serious head injury. Not long after this he had his first epileptic fit. These were to plague him for many years, with sometimes as many as a three or four a day. The family became used to them and were not too concerned and nor was he as long as there was a cup of strong sweet tea and a tot of rum ready by his elbow as the seizure passed. That is until the night he had what they used to call 'a brainstorm'. Clutching a long flaying knife he tried to kill his wife and kids as though they were animals in his slaughterhouse. Thank God no one was hurt, but he was taken away to a colony at Hanbury where he would spend the rest of his life.

His fearsome actions earned him a bit of a reputation, which even extended to his family. My old uncle Joe, Crutcha's grandson, told me he was taken to see him when he was a small boy. In his pleasure at seeing the boy he was fond of, Crutcha kept picking him up and throwing him towards the ceiling. Joe said, 'In later years I could look back and feel sorry for the old boy 'cos he never done me any harm, but at the time I was terrified, so I told my dad I didn't want to go back and I never saw him again.'

As I was brought up mainly among the extended family of the Lees, I soaked up their history and family stories from the moment I was old enough to understand. Every one of them loved to talk and I was always ready to listen. But as with families, there is always a leaning towards one side or the other. Involvement with the maternal or paternal side is rarely down the middle in equal shares. For this reason my memories and knowledge of the Kray side are scant. We learned very little from my father, for though my father's biggest asset as a wardrobe dealer, or buyer and seller of second-hand clothing, was the gift of the gab, at home he wasn't a great one for conversation. At least not on the kind of subject the Lees loved so much – talking of the past.

As much as I do know of the Krays is that they were gypsies. Not tinkers or didicois but true Romanies. The Kray surname suggests they came from those families who travelled through Romania, Hungary and Austria. Why they should have left Central Europe and travelled across the sea to Britain is not known, but as wandering was in their blood it is not surprising that they should gravitate towards what was then the richest capital in the world. That they ended up in the poorest part imaginable could have been due to circumstance, but more likely that as horse dealers the position in the centre of town was perfect for supplying the animals which were as depended upon then as the car and lorry are today. The world of the 1870s into which my grandparents were born was one of exciting change, new inventions and great happenings. But none of this would have any effect on the people who struggled for existence inside this ghetto, shunned by those outside it. But the slum-like conditions and hardships of the area were no worse and possibly better than what the Krays had been used to.

Because of their background my grandfathers Jimmy Kray and John Lee were similar characters, both short, strong, streetwise and very tough – both survivors. As kids they would have helped the family income with a bit of thieving. Nothing serious but it was part of life then, as it always had been and would be right up until and beyond my own childhood. A lump of coal off the back of a passing cart, a bit of fruit from under one of the stalls in Brick Lane or Hoxton Market and, if they were quick on their feet, a loaf of bread out of the window of the baker's. Most of the shops then would hang their wares outside to catch the customer's eye, all securely tied with a bit of string. But what boy didn't carry a knife? A quick slash and there was a teapot, a brush, or a pair of shoes to keep or sell to neighbours. On top of that there would be the legitimate work of helping their fathers, or there would be work to be had like minding or leading horses for tradesmen, pulling handcarts or running errands for anyone who cared to hire their services. When free to pursue their own enterprise, young boys would perhaps collect discarded boxes from the markets, break them into firewood and sell the bundles at a halfpenny each. Anything for a few coppers to put food on the table. All these things when they were less than ten years old. Real childhood in those days probably didn't extend much beyond the age of five.

Without such entertainment as the cinema or television, children's heroes would be those of flesh and blood. Local hard men and villains who could be looked up to and of course boxers; for fighting was in the blood of every man and boy in the East End. How else could you prove yourself as a real man? How else could any of them dream of escaping from the hardship and grinding poverty? Could they become a famous writer like Charles Dickens or an actor like Henry Irving? No, because this was about as likely as flying. But with their fists it was possible to become rich and famous. Sixty or more years later, my brother Ron and I would have the same dream of fame.

It's a reasonable guess to suppose my grandfathers would have followed the careers of heroes such as John L. Sullivan, Jim Corbett and Bob Fitzsimmons, perhaps cutting out pen drawings illustrating their fights from the penny papers. Neither Jimmy nor John ever reached fame and riches with the gloves on but both were known throughout the East End as ferocious fighters. Dad's father earned the title 'Mad Jimmy Kray', because he was all of that. Mad to take on men twice his size that he soon cut down. Mad to take the punishment he did without backing off, and when facing an opponent completely, madly fighting until he'd savagely beaten them.

Grandad Lee was more boxer than fighter and he took the gloves up professionally for some time as a flyweight. Not that he was fussy about staying within this category. At nine stone four, he would take on anyone for a fiver, didn't matter how big they were. He earned his name and reputation on the strength of his right-hand punch which his opponents, after they had been picked up off the canvas, swore they never saw coming. The name 'Southpaw Cannon Ball Lee' might not be in the reference books but it's still remembered in the minds of those who saw him in action. If that makes you think that anyone who can have memories of that famous punch must be very old indeed – think again. He was still using it when he was seventy-five and more than willing to use it at ninety-five!

It's a strange thing that even something like a style of boxing can be passed on to another generation, not by teaching but through the chemistry of the body. I am told that when I was in the ring I took after Grandad Lee and I'm sure Ron would not disagree that his 'steam in and flatten the opposition' came straight from the genes of Grandad Kray.

By the time my grandparents had married and were raising families the facts about their lives become clearer. I can imagine Jimmy Lee was a pleased and proud man when Mary presented him with a son. A man's first-born is special, particularly if it's a boy, for this child would carry the name forward. They would play together, then work together, and with coaching from his old man this lad would realise aspirations that the father hadn't reached – perhaps by taking the boxing world by storm – Cannonball Lee Jr. World Champion. The dream was to be short lived, for cradled in his father's arms little Jimmy went into a convulsion and died. Nan and Grandad had a close relationship and thought the world of each other. But they shared a sense of humour that might have appeared cruel to anyone who didn't know them. Years later Nan would point at Grandad and say with apparent seriousness, 'It was looking at his face that killed that poor baby.'

Around 1900 Joe was born. Money must have been hard to come by because he remembers they were constantly on the move from one room to another. More than once Grandad would give a landlord a good hiding when he got fed up with constant demands for the rent. One time they ended up on the streets without even the money for a night's lodgings. Taking pity on his daughter's plight, her father allowed Mary and Joe to move in with him, but no way was the old man welcome. To the staid old German Jimmy's language and aggressive ways were not acceptable. So while

Jimmy bedded down among the horses he worked with, Joe and his mother lived in unaccustomed comfort for a short while.

One afternoon, as they all sat round the tea table, a neighbour called in and was invited to join them. For a long time young Joe stared with fascination at the man's wispy beard until, unable to contain himself any longer, he patted his mother on the arm to get her attention and said loudly, 'Mum, that man looks like a fucking Billy goat.' Shocked beyond belief, Mary's father said, 'Mary, I suggest you pack your bags and take that child out of this house.' They were back on the streets again.

Their financial position must have improved by the time they decided to have a photographic portrait taken of their son Joe. In those days you would go into a shop and be very formally snapped against a background scene of mountains or a waterfall. They would also supply props to give the picture that extra something. In Joe's case this was a large 'cup and saucer' hat. He kicked up hell and refused to wear it. When the threat of a clip round the ear didn't work, Mary tried bribery. 'Wear the hat for the nice man and I'll buy you something on the way home.' That did it; he couldn't get it on his head quick enough. On their way home Joe chose a toy whip from a stall in Whitechapel Road, and for a while was content to drive imaginary cattle in front of the two of them. However, as they turned into Brick Lane they came across a donkey and cart laden with tin ware: buckets, pots and pans and various other bits and bobs. The driver was in the shop unloading and to young Joe the donkey's rear end was just too tempting to ignore. In a flash he gave the poor unsuspecting animal a stinging crack across the arse. It shrieked in pain and surprise and took off down the lane as though its tail was on fire. Shamed, his mother dragged him down a side turning before the carter spotted them. This from a man, who today, aged ninety-five, still strong and in good health, would have all children exterminated as being cheeky, unruly and beyond the control of their parents.

Gradually the family grew. Joe was followed thirteen years later by John, and then in quick succession May, Rose and my mother Violet. Sitting here now, thinking of how Nanny Lee described her as a child conjures up a lovely mental picture – small and plump with bright rosy cheeks. A happy little girl whom the rest of the family called Doodle. Bit of a dreamer though. If she was sent down the road to buy two pennyworth of pickled herring she would eat the fish on the way home, then with genuine innocence, carefully put the bones on the table. Or she'd be sent down to the shop to fetch a bowl of faggots and pease pudding and then slowly walk home with the bowl on her head pretending it was a hat. One day her mother spotted her from the door and shouted out, 'Don't you dare drop that basin.' She did.

Rose, though, was a livewire, as she would be all her life. She never stood still, always had to be tearing about. One day, scuffing down the road with one foot on the back plate of a little pushchair she ran into the legs of a neighbour four or five doors away. There was a bit of a row and whether the woman raised a hand to her I don't know, but just at that moment Grandad Lee came along. Jimmy wouldn't hit a woman, but as the woman's husband had come out of the house to join in the argument he was soon knocked sprawling on the pavement by that famous left hook. From the door behind him a bull-sized neighbour stepped out, put two punches into Jimmy's back and went back inside. Little Rose stood there, not a bit frightened – she'd seen her dad in action too many times for it to upset her. Roaring his head off Jimmy kicked the door open and in his own words 'Paid him dreadful'.

Jimmy seemed to spend his days teaching someone or other a lesson. When he worked as a pair-horse carman for a firm called Donaldson's he was offloading chests of tea down at Hayes Wharf when one of the horses, bored with standing idle, took a nip at a passing docker. The man picked up a length of wood and belted the horse straight between the eyes. Grandad shouted at him, 'Oi, you bastard, pack it in before I give you the same.' Dockers were notorious for their toughness and without hesitation he shouted back, 'OK shorty, fuckinwell come down and try it,' at the same time grabbing Grandad by the leg and pulling him off the tailgate. Knocked spark out, he was carried into a little factory opposite by some of the women workers. He probably thought he was in heaven when he woke up as he had an eye for the ladies. Uncle Joe told me that when he came home that night his dad's broken face was horrible to look at, but he shrugged off everyone's concern with, 'It's nothing to what his is going to be.' Next day, he went looking for the man, found him and battered him senseless. But that wasn't enough – every time he saw the man after that he attacked him. Nine fights later the docker gave up his job and disappeared. That was Grandad Lee; he could carry a grudge for ever.

When Grandad went after a couple of tiny upstairs rooms in Emming Street, Bethnal Green, he told the landlady who lived downstairs that there was only him, his wife and a boy. Later that day when seven of them moved in, she kicked up hell. 'This ain't on. You wait 'til my ol' man comes home.' When the poor bloke came home from work and was sent upstairs to clear out all these lodgers, he got a good hiding and was flung down the stairs. It must have got smoothed over because they lived there for ages afterwards and got on well with the owners. Not that it was all plain sailing. One afternoon Nan came back from shopping with the three girls, put a match to the oven and blew the place up. Somehow the gas taps had been left on. It's a miracle none of them was killed. As it was, the cooker was wrecked, glass blown out of the window and little May got a cut head.

Life wasn't all bad, though. Because of his boxing Jimmy was a keep-fit fanatic and he would think nothing of cycling to Southend, having a run along the front, then pedalling his heavy, straight-framed Raleigh all the way home. When he could, he'd rope in young Joe and John for the ride but they were less keen and if they saw him tucking his trousers into his socks they'd make themselves scarce double quick.

One day he saw a mate of his pulling a street barrow and he was making hard work of it – puffing and panting. 'What's up with you?' Jimmy says to him. 'I could pull that fucking thing to Southend without breaking into a sweat.' Quick as a flash his mate said, 'Bet you a pound you couldn't.' In those days you could rent a cart for a couple of shillings a day, so next morning Jimmy got up early, hired a cart without saying what he wanted it for, and set off forty miles to the coast. He won his bet and picked up his pound, but a week later he bumped into the cart hire man who said, ''Ere Jim, you owe me fifteen bob for the cart.'

'No, I don't,' said Grandad. 'I only used it for one day, and anyway it had a wonky wheel so I left it.'

'Left it where?' screamed the bloke.

'Southend, all right! Here's your two bob, now piss off.'

Knowing grandad's reputation the man swallowed it but he never let him hire another cart.

Apart from being known all over as a fighting man, Jimmy was a well-known variety entertainer. Variety was very popular in the days before television. The acts were unsophisticated, if not amateurish, but if the customers enjoyed it, that was all that mattered. Jimmy's act was a mixture of strongman, acrobat, daredevil, singer and dancer. This wasn't just a Saturday-night pub turn, but something worth being paid for in theatres all over the place. He'd start off his act with a bit of nimble tap-dancing, follow this with a song or a comical monologue, then he would have a brazier of hot coals brought on stage. Placing a poker into the coals he'd sing another song to stretch out the anticipation of the audience, who all knew what was coming. Then with a drum roll from the pits, the white-hot poker would be pulled out with a flourish and, rolling his eyes and hamming it up, he'd lick the poker as if it was an ice cream to great applause. For his finale, he signalled for bottles and other props to be brought on and a ripple would go through the crowd because this was what he was famous for. This part of the act was always worth seeing no matter how many times it had been seen before. First a barrel would be put down, next to it a tall stepladder and leading up to them a double line of bottles placed neck down. Another drum roll, more showman's banter and starting from a headstand Jimmy'd walk on his hands down the line. He'd keep hold of the last two bottles, then without pausing climb the ladder balanced on their necks. At the top he'd do a somersault and land feet-first into the barrel to deafening applause.

Uncle Joe told me that his dad would often practise that act by jumping out of the upstairs window of the rooms where they lived in Kelday Road. Although he had a standing bet of fifty pounds for anyone who could repeat this trick, he never had to pay it out. Which was just as well, for most of the time the Lees didn't have two ha'pennies to rub together.

It's strange to think he might very well have been on the same bill as turns like Dan Leno, Little Tich and Marie Lloyd, for they all performed in the same theatres as him. Unlike today though, where people go to the theatre and sit quietly until the end, and then they applaud, in music halls such as the Paragon on Mile End Road, the Variety on Pitfield Street and the Pavilion at the Whitechapel Road end of Vallance Road, the audience were in charge. If the act was to their liking they would bring the house down with cheers and shouts. If not, they would shower the stage with specs (over-ripe oranges) or demand the curtain was dropped on the hapless performer. One night Jimmy and his young son Johnny did a turn at the Foresters. They must have been off form because straight away the crowd started to heckle and boo. Great trouper that he was, Jimmy shouted, 'Fuck you then,' and walked off stage, leaving Johnny to face a bigger uproar.

The family love of the theatre was another thing passed down to Ron and me. The Pavilion Theatre at the end of Vallance Road was known in those days as the Drury Lane of the East End. It had the second largest stage in the world and could seat more people than Covent Garden Opera House. From royal boxes downwards, it was decorated with gold-leaf cherubs and rich velvet hangings. Yet in 1940 when Ron, myself and a few other friends discovered this magical place it was boarded up, filthy and disused. What a place though. We'd squeeze through a broken panel round the back, creep laughing and giggling through the darkness under the stage, climb a flight of wooden stairs, then out into the auditorium. I must admit at that age I had no imagination for those who had thrilled the crowds years before, nor was I aware that my grandad Lee might have danced his way across that stage. But I wasn't insensitive to a deep feeling of respect for a place obviously hallowed and haunted by famous people from the past. Saying that, we weren't averse to having a bit of fun there. We would raise and lower the velvet curtains, rummage through discarded stage-clothes that were strewn about and if we found a feathered hat or striking dress-coat we'd put them on and strut about the stage pretending to be actors. My favourite spot was the royal box. I would sit there for ages thinking the King of England sat in this seat.

Bearing in mind that we were only about seven years old the first time we entered the theatre, we thought we'd struck it rich when we discovered paper money strewn all over the place. Imagine how excited we were as we ran home to Mum clutching a small fortune. You've guessed – it was stage money. I can remember being more disappointed for Mum's sake than for my own.

As an adult I took my wife Frances to all the best theatres in London and eventually to La Scala in Milan. But as rich and exciting as they were, none ever filled me with the same emotions as I felt back in the Pavilion as a child. I can honestly say that that experience and Grandad Lee's influence inspired in me a long lasting-love of the stage, actors and all forms of entertainment.

Another place we entered illegally and had great fun in was the back yard of an army surplus store in Dumbridge Road. We called the place Ginger's and once we'd clambered over the back wall it was like entering Aladdin's cave. Everything imaginable that had been needed by the army during and after the First World War was piled up in sheds and under tarpaulins. What we could lift, we pinched. I remember in one shed there were hundreds of real machine guns. In hindsight they would have come in handy later in our lives but we left them there and instead returned time after time to steal bundles of cigarette papers. Years of damp had welded them together into solid blocks and we found they made great missiles when we went on raids against other kids. I can still conjure up the smell of those wartime relics.

At the same time as my grandad Lee was struggling to support his family, on my dad's side, grandfather Jimmy, whom we would always call 'Farvie', married his wife Mary and was under pressure to feed his own family of nine children. Six boys and three girls: our father Charles Davey, Alf, John, Jimmy, Bert, Billy and the girls, Lou, Dolly and Charlotte. His earlier years probably mirrored those of Jimmy Lee. Both fighting men, no doubt their paths crossed sometimes – if not on the streets then very likely in the ring or booths of the local fairs.

Jim Kray had the gypsies' gift of turning fourpence into a shilling using nothing but his silver tongue and street cunning. An asset my father would inherit and improve on. Leaving behind the hard graft and long hours of horse dealing, he went into the business of buying and selling secondhand clothes, which was then known as wardrobe dealing. Anyone with bottle and as little as a ten-bob note could start up in this game. He would study the local paper or pick up on local knowledge as to who had died in the last week. Then he'd be straight round to the family house, offer his condolences and tell them he was just passing and wondered if they had any clothes to get rid of. Which of course they had. This wasn't preying on bereaved widows and widowers, as in those days people treated death with more realism and acceptance. They had no use for the clothes so why not turn them into silver. Only snag was, he would tell them that suits and dresses from someone who has passed on are very difficult to sell – nobody wants them – so will five bob be all right? This logic could be understood by anyone, so more often than not the offer was accepted. Many times he must have left those front doors clicking his heels together because a tidy suit could fetch seven shillings and sixpence on its own.

Unlike most of the dealers who might travel as far as Brighton or Essex, Jim preferred to stay nearer home. Just after the First World War council estates were springing up all over the place and these became his hunting ground – fewer travelling expenses, more profit. Most of the people on these estates were setting up home for the first time, so he hit on the idea of instead of bartering with cash he'd offer china. Being in the know, he could probably buy a set for half a crown or at the most three shillings and sixpence. Plain white with a nice gold rim or the ever-popular blue and white willow pattern. When these were shown to the ladies at the door they'd think they were looking at fifteen bob's worth and wouldn't be able to sort out the clothes quick enough. With temptation like this it wouldn't surprise me if many a husband came home to find his favourite jacket had been 'thrown out'. That was Jim – with his eye for business he'd always see that bit further than anyone else. Eventually he would find that his eldest son, my father, had an aptitude for buying that surpassed his own, so while he set up and sold from a little shop in Brick Lane, he could confidently leave the buying to him.

On my mother's side the family fortune changed suddenly with the death of her grandfather. He'd made a good living with his butcher's shop in Smithfield so there was a nice windfall for his sons and daughters – or should have been. One of my great aunts had married a man who, in the family language, had a bit of a headpiece on him, meaning he was clever. They lived in a posh part of Epsom in a place called Ewell. For some reason this son-in-law became executor of the old man's will, but instead of just dealing with the ins and outs of the paperwork and then handing over the money, he kept it in a sort of trust. When any of the family wanted a bit of cash they would have to go and see him and have it recorded in a book before receiving it. Trouble was, if they got and signed for five pounds, he would alter it afterwards to fifteen. At the end of the day they were swindled out of half of what they were due. All, that is, except that crafty old bugger Grandad Lee. How he swung it no one knows. Uncle Joe told me that one night he came home from work and his dad was sitting at the kitchen table with two hundred gold sovereigns spread out in front of him. Joe's first reaction was, 'Fucking hell, he's robbed a bank.' But he was relieved to learn that the old man had just been to Epsom 'to pick up me legacy'. I tend to think that he swung the executor around his head until he paid up. But however he got the money, he was now ready and financially able to open Lee's Fish Shop.

He knew as much about running a shop and cooking anything more than a boiled egg than he did of space travel, but he couldn't be talked out of it. He got himself a shop near Shoreditch, put flyers all over the place advertising fried fish, soup, faggots and dinners, and away he went. Seven or eight weeks later he went bust and lost every penny. As he would tell anyone who'd listen, it wasn't his fault, 'It was them fucking Jew bastards that undercut [his] prices.' The family tiptoed around him for weeks afterwards and God help any of them who mentioned fish.

It's been said that his family were frightened of him and wouldn't dare lift a fork while he was still carving the joint, but that was the way of fathers in those days. They demanded respect and it was given without any thought of argument. Tough or as strict as he was, he never raised a hand either to his wife or to his children.

East End men had a lot of vanity, which never embarrassed them in the least and he was no exception. Preparing himself to go out he would wind a white silk scarf around his neck, put on his hat, then stand looking at himself in the mirror over the fireplace, humming tunelessly and sucking noisily on his one remaining front tooth. While the others were sitting around the table, Rose would stand in the doorway twisting her face into all shapes and sucking her teeth. Hearing the giggles and spotting her in the mirror, he'd say, 'That's it, go on, girl, take the piss if you ain't got nothing better to do.' He'd say this with a grumpy voice but with a grin on his face because, though he didn't approve of disrespect or being spoken back to, he wasn't so hard that he couldn't join in with the family and laugh at himself occasionally.

He couldn't always see the funny side of a joke. A pal of his called Bill, an old-time boxer and fighter, got himself a job driving a horse-drawn hearse for a local undertaker. He would have looked the business with his top hat and tails, shiny black carriage and two-plumed jet-black horses. Driving past the house with an empty coffin in the back, he saw Nanny Lee sitting outside the front door shelling peas. Not knowing that the old man was about he drew up and shouted down to her, 'Have you laid him out yet 'cos I've come to get him.'

Nanny Lee said, 'It's about fuckin' time.'

Suddenly a voice from inside shouted, 'Gerrout of it you flash bastard, or you'll be the first one to end up in a fucking box.' As big as he was, old Bill nearly fell off the hearse with shock and took off pretty quick. The family laughed about that for years after.

Because of the way his father ended up, rightly or wrongly through drink, Jimmy never touched a drop himself. In fact he hated the stuff and wouldn't have it in the house. Nan was the opposite and loved a glass of whisky. To get round the old man's eagle eye she'd often send the kids out for half a bottle. They would go along with the conspiracy and hide it on top of the high cistern in the outside toilet, hang it in a bag on the fence or tie the bottle to a piece of string so that Nan could pull it up into the bedroom. He never did catch them at it. Uncle Joe said he often had to 'nip round Auntie's' as his mother would call the beer house, and fetch a jug of stout. By the time he got back, Nan would have a poker in the fire, red hot and ready to plunge into the beer to warm and froth it up.

When Grandad worked for Miles and Hyams, they sent him to Lancashire to collect a lorry. As it was brand new it had to be brought down to London to have a cab fitted by specialists in that line of work. It was in the middle of winter, freezing cold and he had to drive two hundred miles with no protection from the elements. He was so cold when he arrived back at Spitalfields that he had to be carried into the office. The guvnor of the firm said, 'There you go Jim,' and stuck his wages into his top pocket and made him drink a glass of whisky 'to warm him up'. On his way home Grandad collapsed, dead drunk, on the cobbles and lay there for over an hour until a copper picked him up. On top of what he'd gone through, while he was spark-out someone had nicked his money. In the kitchen at home was a black range, fire and cooker all in one. He staggered through the door, opened the oven, stuck his head inside and never moved until morning. That was the first and last drink of alcohol he ever had in his life.

Like most East End men, Grandad Lee had a jealous streak in him. One afternoon Nan took young John to the pictures to see a heart-throb of the day, Milton Searles, a screen tough guy. On the way home she got some fish and chips for Jimmy's tea and put them in the oven. When he got home from work she was sitting at the table with a glass of beer in front of her. That wasn't a problem as he didn't class beer as strong drink. What upset him was her going on and on about the film. 'Wasn't he good looking, wasn't he strong.' In the end he jumped up, grabbed the beer and threw it out of the open front door. 'Milton Searles – I'm fed up hearing about him.' Nan wasn't frightened of him, 'Chuck my bleeding beer away, well, you ain't having your dinner,' and she took the fish and chips out of the oven and threw them into the fire. He was so surprised he sat all evening and never opened his mouth.

The Lee family then moved on to Vallance Road. They were growing up, and my uncle Joe, being the eldest, was the first one who went out to work. His schooling, more than the others, had suffered because of all the moving they did when he was little. He didn't start school until he was twelve and that wasn't to last long because with money needed at home he had to leave and get a job. His first job as groom and horse minder was short lived. During an argument with one of the men, Joe, being a chip off the old block, knocked him out cold. The man was carted off to the London Hospital and Joe was laid off.

A few other jobs followed, then he joined his father as a stoker on a big steam traction engine he was driving at the time for a haulage firm in Stepney. While Grandad Lee drove, Joe would shovel coal into the furnace that created the steam to drive the engine. It was also his responsibility to load up the coal back at the depot. If the lumps of coal were too small it would cause a blow through, so on his father's instructions young Joe always filled up with the largest pieces until the manager complained, telling him to take what came, dust an' all. This must have been one of the few times that Jimmy didn't up-end somebody for speaking out of turn. All he did was tell the manager where to stick his engine, called Joe over and they both walked out.

Straightaway they got a similar job with Samuels' over the

river. Joe soon picked up the skills needed to keep a big steam engine going and though he wasn't supposed to, he drove it with his father looking over his shoulder. Then one day his father told him that he'd have to go to work on his own as he had a bit of business to do. He said, 'Any questions, just show them my licence.' Joe filled up with coal and water and set off for Lewisham to deliver his load. What he didn't know was that a few days previously his father must have run into something and bent the steering rods, leaving the front wheels with a mind of their own. He managed to get as far as Blackheath before they seized up altogether, so he got towed into a yard and went home. As Uncle Joe told me once, it might still be sitting there because his dad had laughed and said, 'Fuck 'em, it was a rotten job anyway – we ain't going back.'

Grandad never worried about anyone or anything except himself and his family. He might not have worried too much about the boys because he'd taught them to fight and look after themselves, but when it came to his daughters May, Rose and Violet, he was very strict. He wanted to know where they were going, who they were going with and God help them if they came in later than he'd told them to. In his mind he was looking out for them and doing his best to protect them from what lay outside the door in that tough district. But like all young people, they thought he was a miserable old man out to spoil their pleasure out of spite. So with constant arguments, home life for them all was to become very strained.

My mother had grown from a chubby little girl into a beautiful blonde-haired and blue-eyed young woman. Her sisters were as equally striking and I can imagine that Vallance Road became a magnet for every young man in the district. The road would be as far as they got though, for Jimmy would see them all off in no uncertain way. But the girls were not always under the watchful eye of their father and at the local dances they could let their hair down and enjoy themselves in girlish innocence. The only damper would be the thought of yet another row when they got home – always that little bit later than they should.

3

The Beginning

My mother couldn't have known how drastically her life was going to change the night she set off to a dance in Mare Street, Hackney, where one of the young men stood out from all the others. Smartly suited, dark hair slicked back in the style of the day and with highly polished shoes, his gypsy-like good looks must have set hearts racing all round the hall. But when the band struck up it was Violet he politely asked for a dance, and it was Violet that Charles Kray would see safely home that night, though she would make sure he didn't walk as far as her front door. After that night they spent every spare hour together because they were very much in love. He was proud to have this lovely girl on his arm, and she was proud to be seen with this handsome and confident young man.

Then, as had to happen in a place where neighbours made it their business to know what was going on and then spread the word, Jimmy Lee got wind that an older man of twenty-four was courting his sixteen-year-old daughter and all hell broke loose. She was forbidden to go out with him with the empty threat of a good hiding if she disobeyed. There were tearful arguments and shouting matches between father and daughter until, taking drastic steps for the times they lived in, Violet and Charlie decided to elope and get married. With a ceremony in a registry office and no celebration, they moved into a room in his parents' house in Gorsuch Street off Hackney Road. Her dad raved and swore to the others still at home, 'She's no daughter of mine, I don't ever want to see her again.' But inside he was broken up.

Months after, when he had cooled down, he said to his son Joe, 'Come on, let's go and get our Violi back.' When they got there they could hear loud music from a party that was going on. It took a few knocks before someone they didn't know opened the door and asked them what they wanted. Very politely Jimmy said, 'Could you send my girl Violi out, I want to have a word with her.'

'She's not here, mate,' the person said.

Just then a voice from inside shouted, 'Who is it?'

The bloke said, 'Violet's father – he wants to speak to her.'

Back came the answer, 'Well tell him to fuck off out of it,' and the door was slammed shut in their faces.

Jimmy went mad. 'Fucking bastards, talking to me like

that', all the time kicking the door until his son persuaded him to leave it and come away. He walked home terribly hurt, as though his own daughter had told him to eff off. But the row had nothing to do with her; she had been upstairs too frightened to come down. I don't suppose Jimmy Kray meant what he shouted either, but enjoying the party and with too much drink inside him, he said the first thing that came into his head. But Grandad Lee took the rejection to heart and it upset him for a long time afterwards.

My mother wasn't shunned by the rest of the family though. May and Rose often dropped in to see her and bring her up to date on what had been happening, and when her mum called to see her she always left a few eggs or a bit of meat to help out. Not that Mum and Dad needed helping out, because business was good at that time. Charlie was more enterprising and adventurous in his search for customers to buy from than his father had ever been. Often he was away from home for days at a time as he travelled around the country in search of a deal.

A year after they were married my brother Charlie was born and in a way his arrival was to slowly heal the upset between Violet and her father. This didn't happen straight away but gradually. But with a word here and a word there and a few passed-on messages they eventually began talking again. Things were looking up for all of them, but even better still, with young Charlie less than a year old, Mum found she was pregnant again. The first-born had been a boy – that's how tradition said it should be. That one was for the father. The second, which with a woman's intuition she knew would be a girl, was for her to dress up in pretty clothes and to be close to as only a mother and daughter can. Sadly the baby came prematurely. Leaving Violet on her own, someone rushed to fetch the doctor but by the time they returned the baby was dead. A policeman, who came shortly afterwards as a matter of formality, looked at the tiny dark-haired girl and said, 'Mrs Kray, she is beautiful.' Her name was to be Violet after our mother. Many years later I came across a sad memento of her. Pressed inside a black-edged card was a dried carnation taken from her funeral wreath.

For many months after losing her baby my mother was so grief-stricken that eventually the doctor told my dad, 'If your wife doesn't become pregnant as soon as possible, she's going to lose the will to live and just fade away.' A move to Stean Street just off Kingsland Road initially helped to take her mind off her loss, but when she found out she was not only pregnant again, but expecting twins, it can only be imagined how happy she was and she was soon on the road to recovery.

In the autumn of 1933 I was born, followed three-quarters of an hour later by Ron – both, like the little sister before us, with a full head of black hair. If Charlie's birth broke the ice in her relationship with old Jimmy, ours brought about a complete thaw, and in no time it was like it had always been:

one close, happy family. Twins were rare enough to catch the attention of everyone who saw them and from what I'm told the whole family shared Charlie and Violet's pride.

Our home in Stean Street was in some rooms over a furniture shop, and though my memories of the years spent there are few and hazy, one of the strongest is of playing day after day among the closely stacked tables, chests of drawers and large ornately carved wardrobes. The mind being what it is, looking back it seems as though Ron and I did nothing else but play hide and seek, make little secret camps, and climb daringly through the maze of what today would be valuable antiques. At least mum always knew where to find us. I remember when I was about five or six Aunt Rose saying, 'How would you like to live right next door to me? Then I could take you out every day.' I trusted Rose, but adults can say some funny things, so I looked at Mum but she was laughing and nodding, saying, 'That's right. We're going to move near Nanny Lee.'

Within the week Uncle John had brought his lorry round and helped Dad to load up our furniture and we were on our way to 178 Vallance Road, to the little part of Bethnal Green known as Lee Corner. With Nan and Grandad close by, Aunt Rose and Uncle Bill next door and Aunt May and Uncle Albert next door to them, it seemed that all the people I was closest to were all around me.

The house was a tiny two-up two-down but to a youngster it was a huge palace. That it was damp, crumbling, and shaken day and night by passing trains was of no concern to me – it was a proper house and I felt safe and comfortable there. Dad must have felt settled too because he had hundreds of business cards printed advertising the fact that he bought gold, silver and clothes.

Dad had always liked a drink but now he was in the habit of stopping off for a bit too much on the way home from selling what he'd acquired on the knocker. This took a fair bit out of the cash he'd earned. After squaring Mum up with her housekeeping – because no matter what he did with his money she never went short, he might not have enough left to go out buying on the next trip. So he'd approach a friend of his to ask him to front him up for the week. This was more often than not another dealer by the name of Arthur Harding, a notorious gangster who'd run with and fought against characters like Dodger Mullins, Alfie Hayes, Jimmy Spinks and the Sabini family, who we were more than likely related to. So good was the old man's reputation as a buyer, Arthur never hesitated as he knew his money was safe and would always be returned with a bit on top.

For a while Dad went out in search of secondhand clothes to buy with Uncle John, his brother-in-law. At first John was reluctant because not being so outgoing he hated going from door to door, but he gave in and agreed to take Charlie and two or three others on buying trips in his big old Chrysler. They'd often go as far as places like Bristol, all sharing the expenses. Money was hard to get though and being unable to afford the five shillings to tax the car, Uncle John laid it up for a bit. Arriving home one night he was surprised when Grandad Lee stuck eight pounds in his hand saying, 'There you go, son, that'll keep you going for a while.' When John asked him what it was for, his dad, pleased as Punch, said, 'Sold that old motor for you.' So that was my dad's transport out of the window and he was back on the trains.

By now we had reached school age and it was with lots of nervous excitement and each clutching one of Mum's hands that we were taken around the corner and across Dunbridge Road to Wood Close School. What impressed me most of all were the floors. Strange for a child to notice but in contrast to the cracked faded linoleum we had at home the rich warmth of the highly polished parquet flooring seemed special in some way. Something else that imprinted itself on my young mind was the appearance of many of the other children. While I accepted as normal the fact that I wore sturdy shoes, a warm pullover and, when needed, a waterproof mackintosh, most of my playmates seemed to have a uniform of frayed shirt, shorts cut down from an older brother's trousers, and broken-backed plimsolls. I suppose this was my first glimpse of the desperate poverty suffered in the East End.

I remember telling my mum about these scruffy kids, and although the thought had never crossed my mind she told me never to make fun of them because it wasn't their fault that their fathers didn't have work. Although she wasn't a particularly religious woman, she'd say, 'When you say your prayers tonight, pray for your schoolfriends that haven't got decent clothes and enough food, and for all the poor people in the world.' And I always did what she said. It was tempting to ask God for a red bicycle or a mountain of Indian toffee but I never cheated, even though no one would ever have known. So every night I'd put my hands together and earnestly believe the world would change because of my asking. I never lost the habit and even today still say a prayer for the less fortunate.

I took to schooling like a duck to water. I may not have been top of the class but I was a long way from the bottom. My main highlight of the day was when all the pupils were gathered together in the main hall first thing in the morning to sing such hymns as 'Down in Virginia', 'The Maple Leaf' and 'The Four Leaf Clover'. You'll see the headmaster's choice had a rather international flavour that would have been lost on us kids as we sang our hearts out, accompanied on an echoing piano.

Another daily ritual for us younger ones was the rest period after lunch. We were encouraged to sleep for an hour on camp beds. First, in an orderly line we would collect one of these stretcher-like beds, that by their drab olive-green colour were obviously army surplus from the First World War, and set them out in the hall or, during the summer, in the playground. Then under the supervision of a teacher to enforce a no giggling or talking rule, we'd stretch out and try to sleep.

I was always too full of pent-up energy to consider dozing off, but with a healthy respect for the teacher I'd lie quietly studying the ceiling or watching birds or occasional aeroplanes in the sky.

After that it was back to lessons for an hour or so, with one eye on the round, white-faced clock as I waited for what I enjoyed most, the rough and tumble of playtime. I can't remember anyone ever standing still. Every second of this precious fifteen minutes had to be spent at top speed. We'd chase or be chased over every inch of the yard, whooping and screeching like Indians, only pausing long enough to dash into the run-down toilets for a drink from the old stone sink, before tearing off again. Any child fortunate enough to have brought or stolen an apple on the way to school would be accosted for the core, and he, king for the moment, would gnaw as close to the pips and pith as possible before magnanimously handing it to whoever he might want as a friend. Or more likely to someone he didn't want as an enemy. Hygiene was beyond our comprehension so it was not out of the way to ask a boy or girl for a 'few sucks' on the sweet they were obviously eating by the bulge in their cheek. It says something, that within reason, this was rarely refused.

While the girls whiled away their time with skipping ropes and games that required a lot of sing-song rhyme and handclapping, the boys, when they could stand still long enough, played mock battles – though the fine line between a playful spar and something a bit more serious was easily overstepped.

A punch to the nose a bit too hard, in the spirit of a friendly tussle, could turn laughing gladiators into ferocious animals. Immediately a cry would ripple through the playground, 'Fight, Fight, Fight,' and in moments the two would be surrounded by a howling mob eager to witness a bit of bloodshed but at the same time pleased they were only spectators. As there was always a teacher on playground duty, the fight would be stopped quickly, either by the two having their ears boxed or, worse, dragged off for a few strokes of the cane.

My very first fight was with a bully by the name of George Tappin. He was bigger, older and heavier than I was, but I wasn't intimidated and gave as good as I got. In fact, I was enjoying it until a vicious punch in the face knocked me to the ground. I would've carried on but a shout of 'Teacher's coming' sent us running all ways. When I got home that night my elder brother Charlie, nearly a man of thirteen, took one look at my black eye and said, 'It's about time I taught you how to box.' So with his help, my dad's, and some coaching from my two fighting grandfathers, Ron and myself took our first trained punches towards eventually becoming professional boxers.

In the world outside our little corner of Vallance Road, events were taking place that would soon bring upset and change into all our lives. Remember these things are happening in the months leading up to my sixth birthday, so I can't pretend that I knew what was going on. As far as I could sum things up in my mind, some man called Mr Hitler was going round fighting everybody. Dad showed me a picture of him in the paper and when I said he looked like Charlie Chaplin he laughed and slapped me on the back. Kids at school were saying that Mr Hitler would come over and drop bombs on us, but I didn't believe them. War was declared but life went on just the same as before.

When we weren't at school, Ron and myself would be playing in the street or sharing our company between aunt May and our young cousin Rita, aunt Rose and her son Billy, or pestering the life out of Grandad Lee to box with us or tell us more stories. Dad was still away a lot of the time earning money for us, Mum said, but our young lives were so filled with things to do I can't honestly say we noticed he wasn't there. Like most kids, as long as Mum is there nothing else matters. But slowly things did begin to change. We were all issued with gas masks in a little satchel. These were made of rubber and had a mouthpiece like a duck's beak. Luckily we never had to use them because they smelled funny and made you feel queasy. At school we started practising air-raid drills. A bell would ring and we'd have to march to the concrete shelters that had been built in the yard. The first time we heard practice guns being fired it caused a bit of alarm because we thought Hitler had arrived. On the streets it seemed like there were cars, lorries and soldiers everywhere – but still nothing happened and life went on as usual. Just in case it did, at home we helped Mum stick strips of brown paper on the glass in all the windows and, for night-time, black sheets so no light could be seen. Then the bombing started.

Being too young to have any imagination about the devastation being caused, Ron and myself thought it was exciting as we lay in the double bed we shared and listened to the distant crump crump of explosions. Nothing came near us, so we felt quite safe. We never realised people were dying because of this until Mum told us to pray for the families of all the people who were killed in an accident just round the corner in Mile End Road. Uncle John brought the story home first, though I didn't learn the details until I was older. An air-raid warning had been given on the wireless, then transmission was shut down in case the signal could be used by the enemy for tracking. At that time John was living in Wilmot Street, Bethnal Green, but as he didn't have a lot of faith in the shelter near his home, he decided to make his way to the underground tube station that was under construction a five-minute walk away. When he reached the Salmon and Ball pub, he saw there was a great crowd of people milling outside the station opposite, so he thought he would hold back until it cleared. One of life's awful coincidences caused what happened next. At the same moment as a railway employee opened the large iron entrance gates to the underground, an anti-aircraft gun was fired in Victoria Park. The crowd, thinking it was a bomb, surged forward and down the steps. As no handrails had been fitted yet, it only needed a couple of people to trip in the panic of getting inside, for a chain reaction to set in. As those in the front fell over those who had fallen, more frightened people were being pushed on top of them from behind. Over two hundred people were crushed or suffocated in no time; among them were Dickie Corbett, a boxing champion, Uncle John's trailer-mate from work, his wife, and the wife of Johnny Boxer, a friend of Uncle Joe's. Her baby was saved by being passed over the heads of those still on their feet. It was the first of many wartime tragedies that affected me deeply.

A week later, I was to have a brush with danger myself. A bomb aimed at destroying the railway line behind our house blasted Ron and me from our bed, smashed every window in the terrace and took half the roof away. We ran down the stairs to our parents and brother Charlie who were at the front door looking up the road. Further down Vallance Road we could see a mountainous cloud of dust creeping into the sky from what used to be a large building called Hughes Mansion. Later on we found out that 130 of our neighbours had been killed as the whole place collapsed on top of them. Ron and I were sad that one of the casualties was a midget who always had time for a friendly word with us.

Thankful that none of her own family had been hurt, but still frightened for the safety of her children, Mum decided it was time to join the thousands who were fleeing London.

Inner-London schools had closed anyway, most being taken over as bases for auxiliary forces. But imagine our excitement when Mum said we were going away for a bit of a holiday. We'd had day trips to Margate and Southend, but the only real holiday we'd ever had was when uncle John and his wife Maude had taken us to her mother's boarding house at Clacton-on-Sea. For me the memory of days spent on the beach are hazy as we were only about three, but it stuck in my uncle John's mind. Years later he told me, 'Talk about a handful, you were a right pair of little bastards.'

I'll always remember the day that Mum, Charlie, Ron and myself stood at Euston Station waiting for a train that would take us to Hadleigh in the Suffolk countryside. Clutching our little brown cardboard suitcases which contained our clothes and treasured toys, we were confident because we had our mum, but everywhere I looked were groups of bewildered looking children waiting to be evacuated. Many were crying with the fear of the unknown away from their families, while most had had little brown labels tied to their coats which gave names and destinations, that could be as far away as Norfolk or Scotland. Dad wasn't with us for the journey because he had 'some business to sort out'. What we didn't know was that he'd got his call-up papers for the army telling him to report to the Tower of London. He'd had more than one of these letters and they had all ended up in the fire. Now he was taking the first steps that would put him outside the law for the next twelve years.

My first sight of the house we would be living in took my breath away. It was bigger than four or five houses in Vallance Road and not only did it have a garden as long as our street, it was set in fields and woods the like of which I had only ever seen in picture books. That period spent living in Mrs Styles's mansion in such lush surroundings was the beginning of a love for birds, animals and the countryside that has stayed with me until today.

Brother Charlie, who was then almost fifteen, got a job in a local shop and when he wasn't working I should think he was chasing the village girls. But Ron and I, with nothing else to do but play, were in paradise. All we had known until then were the grimy streets around our home and a tiny backyard. Now we were to experience total freedom in a landscape that stretched as far as the eye could see. Every day was an adventure. With a bottle of lemonade and a bag of arrowroot biscuits, we'd explore for miles around until the fading light drove us home. We'd climb trees or make clumsy fishing rods from sticks, a piece of string and a bent pin, though never once caught a fish. And in the innocence of the time, and ignorant of conservation, we'd search the hedgerows for birds' nests so that we could add another egg to a growing collection. To part the leafy branches of a hedge and discover a woven nest containing four turquoise jewels had a breathtaking excitement that was indescribable for two East End kids. When winter came and the snow fell, Charlie made a sledge and without a complaint pulled us for miles to higher ground, where the three of us would cling together as we sped down snowy slopes, screaming and laughing.

Some of the local boys didn't take kindly to these 'cockerknee' boys who spoke funny. Slight as we were, our boxing lessons were something those country boys had never come across before, so after we'd bloodied a few noses, standing shoulder to shoulder, they became a lot friendlier.

I could have stayed there for ever but even though her sister May was living nearby, Mum was homesick. You can take a person out of the East End but you can't take the East End out of the person – that's how it was with her. She missed the closeness of the family, the streets and people she had grown up among, and no doubt she missed her own mother. What was heaven to us boys was completely alien to a woman who had never known anything but London life. Another justification for moving back was the rumour that the whole of the south was to suffer saturation bombing. If nowhere was safe we might as well face what was coming in familiar surroundings.

As the train taking us home left Ipswich far behind, Ron and I made a whispered pact that when we were rich and famous boxers we'd come back to Suffolk and buy a house as big as Mrs Styles's and all the family could come and live in it. Many of our childish dreams came to nothing, but this dream was one we never lost sight of and twenty years later we were to return.

Back home, a year or so older, an inch taller, and filled out on good country food, we were ready to explore further afield than we had been allowed to before. What we found was an area equally as exciting as the countryside but in complete contrast. No trees, but broken buildings everywhere for climbing in and around. No fields, but acres of brick and rubble bombsites to scramble over and dig into. How any of us weren't killed is a miracle, as the bricks became hand grenades and we became fearless Tommies blowing up the Nazis. I became one of the first casualties in our make-believe war when a German, in the shape of our cousin Billy Wiltshire, scored a direct hit on my head with a brick grenade. With blood running down my face from a long cut on my head, Ron and Billy walked me home. As soon as Mum saw me and before she could say a word, Billy said, as quick as a flash, 'Alfie Miller did it.' What Mum said she'd do to Alfie if she caught hold of him I needn't say, but I was taken to the London Hospital just round the corner where I had six stitches put in the wound. I never liked deceiving Mum and I hadn't told her a direct lie, but I was pleased that I had not let on that Billy was to blame. Even then 'grass' was a dirty word.

Our cousin Billy was an absolute bastard to us, yet strangely enough we never held any animosity towards him. Because he was older than us we just accepted the treatment he handed out. If ever a kid was destined to end up on the rope it was him. Yet later in life he went into the armed forces and served overseas. This seemed to be the making of him for with his National Service behind him he became a changed man, got a job in Covent Garden and settled down to lead a respectable life with his wife and family. If we'd been told that when he was younger, we wouldn't have believed it possible. He was the wildest kid in the neighbourhood and there was nothing he wouldn't do. I've seen him jump from a building so high you'd be afraid to look in case he was smashed to pieces – which he never was. One time he was walking down Mile End Road with his cousin Joe, who was nearer his age than us, when passing a shop he picked up a large toy motor car. He must have known he couldn't get away with it, but that wouldn't have stopped him. When the shopkeeper gave chase Billy turned round, threw the car at him and knocked him flying. This kind of behaviour was typical of our cousin Billy.

When not tormenting shopkeepers, Billy took to playing tricks on his younger cousins, namely Ron and me. In the type of house we lived in there was no such thing as a bath-room. The flushing toilet was in a little brick shed out in the yard and hanging on a nail beside it was a large galvanised bath. When the bath was needed it was brought indoors and filled up with kettles of water. The alternative to exposing yourself to anyone who happened to walk in the front door was the public baths in Cheshire Street, which was only fifty yards from our house. For a few pennies you could get a nice hot bath in a private cubicle. But if cousin Billy spotted us going in he'd wait until I was undressed and in the bath, then climb over the cubicle wall, spring down and hold my head under the water. Once he'd got me half drowned and cough-ing and spluttering he'd go next door and do the same to Ron.

He seemed to have a thing about suffocation. Half the time Billy was out of work and so he'd lie in bed until dinner time if he could get away with it. If I crept next door to no. 176, sneaked upstairs and woke him up, he'd grab my hair, push my head under the blankets and hold me there until I was turning blue. As an adult it horrifies me to look back at the way we were treated by him, but as lads it was just part of life and in many ways possibly toughened us up, because no matter what he did we never let him know he'd hurt or upset us. Sometimes that took unbelievable will power.

For weeks Ron and I had saved every penny we'd earned or had been given. A penny here and there from Mum or Aunt Rose, perhaps threepence from Grandad Lee, until the big day when we had two shillings and sixpence – just the right money to buy a beautiful cowboy stagecoach we'd seen down the market. It had spoked wheels that turned, a canvas cover and a little black and white horse between the shafts. We had just got settled in the backyard to play with it when Billy climbed over the fence and said, 'I've got a good idea.' He didn't hang about to see if we agreed whether his idea was good or not, but set to burying the toy in a pile of soil then bombarded it with bricks until it was smashed to pieces. If we had told Mum or aunt Rose about it he would've been in trouble, but as usual we kept our mouths shut.

Despite his behaviour, it seemed that whatever he wanted to do we followed. Like the time the three of us and our friend Ronnie Gill set off from Bethnal Green Station for a day's camping at Chingford. This was a great adventure that Ron and I had looked forward to for ages. Once we got there and after a long walk to find a suitable spot, we pitched the tent. I had just climbed inside and was trying to decide whether to be an explorer or an Indian for the rest of the day when Billy pulled up all the pegs and dropped the tent on top of us shouting, 'Fuck this camping game, c'mon we're going home.'

During those early days of my childhood, London was taking a battering. There was one period of time, probably the all-out offensive known as the Blitz, when the bombers came every night for two solid months. It was so regular that we got used to it. Hard to imagine that explosions, death and destruction could become part of life but there must be limits to prolonged fear, so eventually you get used to it. The shelters under the arches in Dunbridge Street became a second home to us. I hope children never again have to witness what we did, yet at the same time it was exhilarating to experience history in the making – a fact I would not be aware of until looking back years later.

While I'd been living in the country I'd seen what to my townie eyes was an amazing sight. In broad daylight a large brown tawny owl (looked up later in *The Observer's Book of Birds*) was being chased backwards and forwards by a mob of smaller birds. It never tried to retaliate, just ducked and weaved to escape them. This incident came right back to me as I stood at the entrance to the shelter and watched an enemy bomber being chased by our own aircraft. Another time I watched a dog-fight in the sky between a Messerschmitt and a Spitfire. Before I was dragged inside I saw the German plane peel away and spin downwards in a trail of black smoke. Where it came down I don't know, but I cheered at the death of the Nazi pilot. I told Mum what I'd seen but I didn't tell her that I'd cheered because I knew she wouldn't approve. Only a few days before Ron had told her he prayed that Hitler would be run over by a bus, but she had told him, 'Doesn't matter who it is, never pray for something like that.' Mum had so much generosity and goodness in her she wouldn't know how to hate anyone – no matter who they were.

Ordinary bombs, if there can ever be such a thing, make a high-pitched whistle as they are falling, but the sound we all dreaded most was four or five seconds of silence. From across the channel would come the pilotless V1 flying bombs. You could hear the doodlebug droning across the sky, then the engine would cut out and those moments until the ear-splitting explosion would seem like an eternity, as you held your breath and hunched your shoulders, bracing for impact.

Although it was a difficult time for everyone, we did to try to make the best of it. During the day when there was no fear of raids, us kids would collect twisted shards of shrapnel from these and other bombs, and also the long streamers of silver foil that were dropped to blind the radar systems. Foil or shrapnel, one piece is very much like another, but that never stopped us searching the rubble or digging it out of walls with a penknife. I must have had a sackful before I moved on to other things.

Uncle John would make us laugh when he came round our house for a cup of tea, saying he must have a homing device somewhere on his lorry because the bombing seemed to follow him around the country. He was a heavy goods driver and kept produce and artillery moving around the country so he was never called up for service. He was in Coventry when it was almost blitzed to the ground, Southampton and South Wales when they faced their worst bombing and Barry Island when the oil refineries were blown up and destroyed. 'Imagine how I felt when I was carting a full load of ten-ton bombs and Jerry starts dropping a few of their own all around me,' he said.

The war also seemed to give Grandad Lee a new lease of life. Nearly seventy and stronger than men half his age, if the choice was his he'd have signed up for the duration. As it was, he settled for being the self-appointed entertainment manager of the air-raid shelter. Old trouper that he was, all he needed was a stage, which he knocked up from Uncle John's lorry pallets, and of course an audience, captive or otherwise. What it must have been like in a shelter with nothing to do but worry about where the next bomb was going to fall, I can't imagine, but in ours it was music hall every night. Grandad Lee sang, danced and tumbled, and like he'd done with his own son Joe many years before, he'd give each child a turn of sitting on a small chair and being balanced on a broomstick placed on his chin. In return each child had to do a party piece. When it was my turn I'd copy Grandad and do a tap dance and Ron could always be relied on to sing a song. When it came time to climb into the little bunks we slept in, I'd lie there full of pride that the man everyone was clapping and cheering was my grandad.

One night a warden stuck his head in and said he'd heard German paratroopers had been seen dropping out of the sky. Straight away my old grandad was ready to go out and round them up on his own. Mum and Rose talked him out of it, saying he was needed here to look after us lot. And obviously it turned out to be just a rumour after all. In any case, Grandad had done his share for the country back in the First World War, when he was in the Flying Corps, the forerunner of the Royal Air Force.

The Battle of Britain was really the end of the war for us at home. It still went on abroad but we didn't have to suffer any more bombing raids, so could think of getting back to normal. Normal for us boys meant carrying on with our education, and soon we were enrolled in Daneford Road School. Again, as with infant school, I took to the learning process with great enjoyment.

For an East End boy who years later would be referred to almost daily in the media as 'Evil Killer' or 'Gangland Slayer' my childhood was probably more normal and more innocent than that of many of my contemporaries. At home, respect and thoughtfulness for others was taught by example by the family around me and quite naturally I carried this philosophy with me into the wider world. So school was no problem as I didn't dream of kicking against authority in the form of teachers. In fact, I joined in every activity with enthusiasm. The headmaster of Daneford Street School was Mr Holloway, but the day-to-day school policy was run by the principal teacher Mr Evans, a big man full of humour. When interviewed some twenty-five years later, Mr Evans said of Ron and myself, 'Those twins were the salt of the earth. Nothing was too much trouble for them and they never refused to help out.' Because of his own interest in rugby, he encouraged all forms of sport above all else and in no time had me playing in the position of right half in the football team. Again I dreamed of being famous and in my mind saw myself scoring the goal that would win the World Cup.

I collected cigarette cards that depicted my favourite players, such as Stanley Matthews, Frank Swift, Tommy Lawton and the Compton Brothers. I would stand outside a tobacconist's and politely ask the men coming out for the card in their cigarette packet, which was usually handed over with a grin, or else I would search through empty packets thrown in the gutters.

Respectful of my teachers I might have been but complete angel I was not. I felt the sting of the cane on more than one occasion. Whatever I was caned for needn't have been very serious, for in those days just being five minutes late for school could earn you a couple of strokes. Teachers back then had the idea that they could knock sense into one end by belting the other. This was accepted in the sense it was given and no grudges were held on either side. Today I can look back with affection and respect for Mrs Peacock, Mr Hawkins, Mr Evans and Mr Holloway.

Considering that Ron and I had a deal going with our headmaster, surprisingly I never felt I should receive special treatment from him. As Uncle John was driving produce all round the country this put him in the position of procuring various goods that because of wartime rationing the ordinary person couldn't get hold of. Usually at night he would be up at Vallance Road bringing in such things as eggs, pork, bananas and sacks of sugar. With Mum's permission we would make up smaller bags of the sugar, take it to school and give it to him. A week later he would hand us back jars of homemade blackcurrant or strawberry jam which his wife had made. A rare treat and the first bit of illegal wheeling and dealing we undertook.

Respect for my elders took a knock back when we first became involved with the police. Though East Enders have always had a traditional wariness or outright dislike of the law, our family was not one of those who taught their lads to vilify the uniform, no matter what their own views were. I can remember at infant school being surprised to hear other five-year-olds sneeringly talking about 'fucking coppers' and 'Old Bill bastards'. To me the local policeman with his domed hat, heavy cape around his shoulders, and big solid bicycle was a friendly enough figure who saw us across the road or, as on one occasion, picked me up after I had fallen and skinned both my knees. This conception was blown away one night when Ron and me were shaken out of a deep sleep by two policemen demanding to know where our father was. Mum had already explained to us that because Dad wouldn't go to war and kill people the police wanted to lock him up. So pre-warned we sat on the edge of the bed rubbing our eyes, yawning and swearing 'Scout's honour' he didn't live with us any more. This wasn't completely untrue, but being a deserter on the run his visits to Vallance Road were few and far between while the heat was on. We knew that he was lodging with a pal of his, Bob Rolfe, a professional villain, but thumbscrews wouldn't have got us to tell anyone.

It wasn't so much what the police did but how they did it. We could be sitting having our dinner and the next minute a copper would come walking through the front door and start searching cupboards and under beds and upsetting Mum while he was at it. Knowing we were all related they'd search the other houses as well. One time Uncle John got a knock on the door. He opened it and a copper said, 'I'm looking for a deserter. Can I come in?' John said, 'Help yourself, you won't find anyone.' The copper rushed past him so fast he slipped on the mat and went arse over head along the passage. He picked himself up, put his helmet back on, and turned over every room in the house. When he went out in the yard John followed and there was law everywhere. There was nowhere to hide in the yard except under the tin bath or in the toilet. But as the copper walked towards it a sergeant next door shouted, 'Over 'ere quick.' Again, brain working faster than his feet, he fell clean over the fence. Just then John heard a voice inside the toilet whispering, 'Fuck me, that was close – get me out of here.' It was Dad. John nipped round the corner, got his lorry and drove up to the front door. The law was still out the back of Auntie May's, so Dad wasn't seen as he shot out of the toilet, jumped in the cab and was driven away – another one of many close shaves.

Dad wasn't the only one on the trot as they called it. Aunt Rose next door, who was divorced from her husband Bill, had a couple of blokes hiding out in her house for ages. The word deserter has always had cowardice associated with it – someone too yellow or too frightened to fight. But without exception the men who used Lee Corner as a safe hideout would have and could have taken on the German Army single-handed if they'd wanted to. What you have to understand is what I said about myself in the beginning. You have to look at their background and roots. The East End might as well have had a wall built around it because in terms of government help and interest it was shut off from other areas and those within the boundaries could either get out or get on with it. All of a sudden these men were ordered to give up hard-won jobs, leave their families to survive without a man to support them, and face possible death – all for a King and Country that had never given them a second's thought before. I know that every man that was called up, no matter where he lived, was in the same boat but the difference was that the East Ender had the bottle to say, 'Fuck the army.' Who could blame them for refusing? Certainly no one round our streets. I never felt ashamed of my father then and have never done so since. I understood.

4

Neighbourhood Watch

It was a different world that I grew up in. When I watch television in the recreation room I am amazed when I see what's on offer for the kids of today, particularly the adverts as Christmas approaches. Don't get me wrong, I think it's great that children now have so many exciting things and don't know what real want and hunger are, but what a contrast to fifty years ago, which is no time at all in the scheme of things. A child today might ask for a colour television for their bedroom or a state-of-the-art computer. Us kids could expect and be overjoyed to find a shiny red apple, a handful of nuts and some sweets in our Christmas stockings, and for a main present a football or a pair of roller skates. We were old enough to want a brand new bicycle but wise enough not to set our sights too high.

These days of paper packaging that must use up acres of rainforest make me think of how we used to buy household items and sweets. Many things were sold loose then. For washing our hair Mum might send us down the shop for a pennyworth of soft green soap, and the shopkeeper would deftly form a cone from a piece of paper, pop the soap in and fold the top over. A twist of tea would be bought in the same way. Jam, when we weren't getting it from Mr Holloway, was collected in a jar and then used again and again for refills. Fish paste was collected in a cup and salt broken off a large block.

It was the traders who came round the doors that gave London the colour I remember so much. The muffin man ringing a large brass bell as he pedalled up the street behind a large box fitted to his tricycle, calling out, 'Muffins – fresh muffins – two a penny.' The ice cream man had a similar set-up with bike and box, but he'd have 'Stop me and buy one' painted in bright colours across the front. Another fella would sing his advert, 'Salt, mustard, vinegar, fly papers – catch 'em alive.' It had a catchy little tune and would bring all the old girls running out.

Black or Asian people were a rare sight in the forties, and we'd stare in fascination when a figure in a turban turned up on the doorstep. In broken English he would try to sell Mum bright silk ties, headscarves and things to hang on the wall. We kids were more interested in what the other black man sold because he was the Indian Toffee Man. Whether the name came from the confection or from his place of birth

I've no idea, but Indian Toffee was something like candy floss. We had a fondness for sweets and I remember one in particular, stick jaw, a lump of that in your mouth and you wouldn't be able to talk for half an hour.

The dog winner man was another regular on the corner of Vallance Road. He would collect a bundle of single sheets listing all the previous night's dog racing results from stadiums like Whitechapel, Hackney or Catford. His wage would be the penny or tuppence he stuck on top of each one and he probably earned himself ten shillings or so because no gambler wanted to wait until the newspapers printed the results the next day. My dad, or the Old Man as we called him, often said, 'Do us a favour, Reg – nip down and get me a dog winner, I feel lucky.' Sometimes there might be a printer's error and then all hell would break loose.

At that time there was no such thing as betting shops. If you wanted to lay your money on a dog or a horse, the only legal way was to place your bet at the track. To get round this the bookies would have runners who would take your bet in the pub or street. These fellas stuck out like a sore thumb with what seemed to be a standard uniform of long coat and pork-pie hat. Because of the occupational hazard of being lifted by the law, these men were never still. Like nervous birds they were always looking over their shoulders.

When they legalised gambling Grandad Lee thought he'd have a go, even though up until then he'd never had a flutter in his life. Because he didn't have a clue about filling in slips and what he should be doing, it was a safe bet he'd make a mistake on the form. When he checked the results he found he had won thirty shillings and rushed down to Danny Levy's to collect. When he got there Danny said, 'Sorry Mr Lee, you backed a loser. Better luck next time.' Grandad went up the wall. 'You bastards ain't doing me out of my winnings, I want it now.' Then he started throwing punches. A couple of blokes pulled him off and got him out of the shop with Danny Levy shouting, 'You'll be getting a visit from Jimmy Taylor if you come round here again causing trouble.' Taylor was a local hard man who worked for the bookie. When Grandad told his son, our Uncle Joe, he went straight round to sort out the bookie for threatening his father. Of course, then he found out the true facts. Levy, who was a decent sort of bloke said, 'Joe, I only mentioned Jimmy Taylor in the heat of the moment. I wasn't going to follow it up. I'll tell you what I'll do. Your old man's got it all wrong; his horse wasn't in the first five but I don't want to fall out with your family, so to keep the peace I'll pay him out of my own pocket.' They shook hands and Joe took the money back to his dad and put it on the table. Grandad looked at and said, 'There you are, fucking robbing Jew bastards got to get up early to get one over on me.' Joe didn't try and explain; it wasn't worth the effort.

Grandad wasn't the only one who could get a bit stroppy. Nan could be a handful if she thought she'd been wronged. A coalman who'd been sacked from his round tried the oldest trick in the book. He called on Nanny and asked to be paid for half a hundredweight of coal that he had delivered. The door to the coal-cupboard was set in the outside wall, so it was possible to empty the coal in without the customer being aware. But she knew the coal-hole was empty so she set about him with her stick and chased him up the road. Another time she had a row with a neighbour while she was scrubbing the front step and ended up throwing the bucket of soapy water over the woman's head.

As well as being a bit mouthy, Nan didn't mind pinching a few things to help feed her family. When they lived in Kelday Road there was a dairy opposite that kept its own cows. They sold other things as well and what Nan would do was go in carrying two metal jugs. She'd get milk in one then use the other to nick anything that was small enough to fit into it. Eventually the owner, who wasn't stupid, said to Aunt May, 'You girls are all right, but I don't want your mother in here no more 'cos she's robbing us blind.' Nan didn't feel guilty about being caught she just said, 'Fuck 'em, I'll do me shopping somewhere else.'

Another time Uncle Joe walked down the shops to meet her and carry her shopping home. He looked in all the shops until he came to the baker's where he could hear a lot of effing and blinding going on. He opened the door and there was his mother pelting the owner with fresh bagels. While she was choosing what she wanted she'd been squeezing all the rolls to make sure they were fresh – that was until she was told to either buy them or leave them alone. That was all that was needed for her to blow her top and by the time Joe pulled her out there wasn't a roll left in the tray. The way Nan and Grandad carried on didn't mean they were being cantankerous for its own sake but they had known hardship all their lives and had grown up in an area where you got nothing without fighting for it. Softness was seen as weakness in the East End and only those prepared to stick up for themselves and family were the ones to survive.

Like all the houses in Vallance Road, Nan's was overrun by rats and mice that came from the railway yard opposite. They didn't bother her, she'd just flick a duster at them and say, 'Go on, fuck off out of it.' Or before she'd pour out a cup of tea she'd blow in it in case mice had got there first. It was from her I got the lifetime habit of drinking strong tea. If I just popped in for a moment and said I couldn't stop she'd say, 'What's the matter, don't you like my tea.' There would always be a large metal teapot stewing away on the trivet by the fire and she'd just keep topping it up. I picked it up once and noticed it was quite heavy. I took the lid off and found it was nearly filled to the brim with tea leaves.

I was sitting talking to her one day, while she dusted round the room and when she lifted the cushion from Grandad's chair, to plump it up, underneath were two flattened mice. When he came in she said, 'Look what you've been and done to them poor mice.' He said, 'Blow me, I've only sat on Bernard and Aubrey.' He'd seen them so often he'd given them names!

Grandad wouldn't go near a spider, yet he'd pick up a rat with his bare hands. One teatime a man knocked on the door and said, ''Scuse me, Mrs Lee, but I just saw a rat run in your front door.' Nan told Grandad and he said, 'Tell it to hang on, I'm having my tea.' By the time he was finished it had got upstairs and was running round the bedroom. He went up after it and two minutes later he came down the stairs holding the screeching rat by the back of the neck. He walked straight out of the door and for a laugh terrorised some girls walking past, before he killed it in the gutter. Every time he saw those girls after that he'd say, 'Come 'ere a minute I want to show you something' – but they never hung about long enough to see if he was joking or not.

As we all lived on the same road, I spent a lot of time at my Nanny and Grandad Lee's house when I was little. It was a bustling house, full of people and excitement that thrilled me as a young boy. Of all the characters who were in and out of there, one impressed and inspired Ron and me more than any other, and that was the boxer Ted 'Kid' Lewis. When we first got to know him he'd been retired for about fifteen years but at fifty he was still a legend. To listen to him talking of the old days and describing the fights he'd had and then squaring up to him in a friendly spar was like a youngster today shaping up to Muhammad Ali. Born at the top of Brick Lane, his real name was Gershon Mendeloff, and he'd started his career at the Wonderland Theatre opposite the London Hospital in Whitechapel Road, a place where most

Jewish fighters headed for to get a foot on the ladder. From what he told us, his technique was a mixture of old-style prize fighting and modern boxing skills. In twenty years he went from cabinet maker to World Champion. On the way he had won three British, two Empire and three European titles before taking the World Title from Jack Britton in Boston, USA. And now that stocky, dark haired, broken-nosed man who'd taken North America by storm, was in Nanny Lee's kitchen throwing mock punches at us.

On the wall out in the yard Grandad had fixed up a mattress which he told us was what all the old-time boxers used. With soft red brick he'd drawn the rough figure of a man with arrows pointing to different body parts we should concentrate on. Chin, forehead, solar plexus, lower ribs and so on. We'd often practised on the mattress, so when he suggested we show Mr Lewis what we could do, we shot outside and knocked the stuffing out of it. I'll never forget him standing there saying, 'Keep that guard up, punch with both hands, keep on your toes.' Then afterwards saying, 'You boys have got what it takes, you'll go far.'

This encouragement from our idol was enough to get us honing our boxing skills. We'd already joined the boxing club at school, under Mr Bell, and were filled with enthusiasm, but with such praise from a World Champion we felt nothing could hold us back. How could we go wrong? We were boxing at school and boxing in a makeshift gym upstairs at home. We also boxed at a youth club near Spitalfields Market called the Vallance Club. This was run by Mr Davis, a really nice Jewish fella who also happened to be a midget. I believe it's wrong these days to use that term, but that's what he was and without embarrassment that's what he called himself. His wife and daughter were equally small. What impressed me was how he dressed. He might have been small but you never saw him in anything but a sharp tailored suit, shirt, tie and highly polished shoes. He had a reputation as a judo expert, which must have been an asset against potential piss-takers.

The youth club, based in the crypt of a well-known church, had table-tennis, snooker and various other activities that included boxing training by another Jewish fella by the name of Bill Gates. Until we got kitted out in proper gear we used to fight in scruffy old plimsolls and shorts made from cut-down women's knickers, which will give you some idea of the underwear fashion of the times. It was a rough little club, but it had a good atmosphere where everyone mixed in together. One of the boys I became very friendly with was an Indian who always wore a turban, even when he was fighting. Before I got to know him better I think I palled up with him out of novelty, because not many kids at that time could boast a mate quite so exotically dressed.

The gym at home was first set up by brother Charlie for his own use, but as he knew he was shortly joining the navy he let us use it – then allowed us to take it over altogether. Mum must have been a saint to put up with the noise above her head, especially when half a dozen mates would come round and join in. But she never complained – just kept us supplied with lemonade and biscuits.

A lot of my friends came from homes where a slammed door or a too-loud wireless could earn them at least a bollocking from the old man, or at worst a clip round the ear. So to come round to 178 and let off some steam without getting into trouble was outside their experience. Mum's capacity for love and friendliness won over every kid that came through our door. Even today I get visits from friends who never fail to remember her with the greatest affection. A typical example is that of James Aish, who is still a good friend of Ron's and mine. In later years Jim became a professional villain and, surprisingly for his size and weight, an unbeatable bare-knuckle fighter. Never judge a man by the lifestyle that circumstances forced him to take up. On a recent visit he told me that he had put his criminal past behind him, joined Mensa and started a career as an artist. He gave Ron and me a portrait of our mother that was so realistic it brought tears to my eyes. He also said that putting brush to canvas on this painting was an emotional experience for him as he remembered our mother's small acts of kindness that were to remain so large in his mind for the rest of his life. Like the time he was playing in the street outside our house. His family, like so many then, was struggling to make ends meet. There was food on the table, but no money left over for much else. So there's young Jim playing out in a November drizzle wearing a summer shirt, when Mum called him over and gave him a warm roll-neck jersey. Being a lot younger than me I can't say that he was a special friend at the time; in fact, I don't think he'd even been in our house. But to Mum he was a child in need and that's all that mattered. On another occasion she noticed one of his friends tying string round the toes of his shoes to keep the soles from flapping open. She called the kid over to the door and gave him a pair of socks and a pair of almost new white plimsolls. What impressed Jim more than anything was the fact that Mum also gave the boy a tin of shoe whitener so that he could keep them looking nice. On top of that, every one of about seven kids got a big lump of bread pudding. Of course that started something that anyone else's mum might have regretted. Because whenever the boys were hungry, which was most of the time, one or other would say, 'Let's go and play outside Mrs Kray's,' and without fail out she would come out with a slice of bread and jam, bread pudding or biscuits for all of them. I suppose with the money that Dad was earning with his gold and clothes buying, plus brother Charlie bringing in a wage, by the standards of the East End our family was better off than most. That didn't mean there was anything to spare, but Mum would rather go short herself than see others go without. In the same way, when she was a girl, her mother, Nanny Lee, would dish up the main meal for the family then potter around the kitchen while they were eating, saying, 'I'm not hungry.' The truth was there wasn't enough for everyone. Often too, that main meal might only be a bowl of rice with a tiny lump of jam in it or a couple of slices of bread with sugar sprinkled on it.

Mum cared for us so much that when I brought trouble home at the age of ten, her tears hurt more than any flogging could have done. It was summertime and Ron, Alfie Miller and I decided we would spend a day at Chingford. Remember this was fifty years ago and then, unlike today, we could be in unspoilt countryside within a short walk from the station. Each of us carried a few sandwiches, a bit of cake, a bottle of water and some sherbet powder to mix in it. The sweeping fields and woods were a kid's paradise. We searched little streams for fish, climbed trees, fed some horses with our bread crusts, and as I'd taken my slug gun with me, whooped and hollered up and down the grassy slopes as we played cowboys and Indians. By four o'clock we'd run out of food and were worn out, so we set off for home. On the train journey back to Liverpool Street, typical kids – we didn't know what to get up to next. We fought and wrestled each other, bounced on the seats and Ron and I lifted Alfie up and stuck him in the netting luggage holder for a laugh. Then I had the bright idea of taking a pop at the irresistible targets flashing by the window with my slug gun. The gun was a .177 Diana air rifle, and was one step up from being a toy. Short black pressed-steel barrel with a light coloured wooden stock, it had the velocity of a peashooter. It could make a decent twang if it hit a metal sign or post, and that would be good enough for us. Not that we expected to see or hear the slug hitting its target, because by that time we'd be half a mile up the track, but it was good fun. That was until we stepped off the train and were immediately collared by two large official-looking men – railway detectives. What could I say: I was still holding the rifle. If I'd known what was coming I could have thrown it out of the window, but instead I was caught red-handed. The biggest man took the gun from me and said, 'Well, Billy the Kid, you won't be needing this in Borstal.' We were taken to an office, made to sit on a hard bench and then, one by one, questioned by these two bullies while a statement was taken.

Can you picture the three of us? Ten years old, scruffy and dishevelled from playing all day, and all thoroughly frightened by the threat of Borstal. Young we might have been, but we'd heard plenty of stories, from older boys who'd been away, of how tough these places were. But worse was to come. Instead of letting us go we were to be escorted home. Alfie was taken in a separate car; we were put in the back of a large Wolseley and driven off to Vallance Road. Aunt Rose and Mum were having a cup of tea when we arrived, and I can still picture their faces when the railway detective told them we would have to appear in court for dangerously discharging a gun in a public place. I think that if I'd hurt someone or been caught stealing I could have accepted the heavyweight treatment we were being subjected to. Ten or not, I knew that if you were caught breaking the law you had to swallow it, but all we were guilty of were childish high spirits and for that we had the threat of being sent away hanging over our heads for a month. Mum was very quiet for those four weeks, and not once did I hear her singing 'Somewhere over the Rainbow' as she often used to when washing up or dusting the front room.

On the specified day we made our way to Toynbee Hall Juvenile Court, a large building at the bottom of Commercial Road. Aunt Rose came along to give Mum moral support, but as soon as we were taken into the large room used as a court they couldn't hold back their tears. After deliberations that seemed to go on for hours, we were given a stern lecture, bound over to keep the peace and allowed to go. Mum and Aunt Rose cried all the way home, but this time because they were happy.

I felt nothing but hatred for the police, railway or not, and the establishment that had put me and my family through a month of emotional hell. In my mind they had become and would remain THE ENEMY. My young mind couldn't comprehend such a thing as the establishment, but later on I would realise that this experience was my first conflict with those faceless powers-that-be, a conflict that was to become greater. These days, though, with a bit more wisdom and tolerance, I've made my peace with the law and no longer see myself in conflict with it.

Up until about that time, Ron and I would cross the road rather than face confrontation or be drawn into a fight. Nothing to do with being frightened of the opposition, because we were both pretty confident in ourselves. It was more like we didn't feel we had anything to prove with unnecessary violence. That changed one day when we were playing by the boating lake in Victoria Park. My memory is vague about what we were doing, probably floating twigs or empty cigarette packets in the water as boats. Next minute five kids of about our own age came along and started taking the piss. Being twins made us different enough to stand out. We looked alike and we thought alike so we had no need to confer before attacking the five as one person. If we'd carried more weight they would've been seriously hurt. As it was, four of them got bloody noses and bruised chins, while the fifth took off before we got to him. The others didn't stay long either. Once they got what they took to be a safe distance from the two of us, they stopped and shouted to us, 'We'll get our gang on to you.' As there was five of them I'm not sure how many they felt were needed to sort us out. This was our first victory over greater odds – it was a good feeling.

A few days later Ron had a fight with another kid at York Hall Baths in Bethnal Green. I don't know what he said to Ron, all I saw was the other fella get a vicious right to the head that split his eyebrow open. It doesn't take much blood in water to look like a murder, and there was a bit of a panic around them until the not so cocky kid was dragged out bleeding and crying.

Because of our involvement with boxing, we thought of

fighting as squaring up, sticking to a set of rules, and punching our way out of trouble, no matter how many we were up against. We were good sportsmen but perhaps we were naive in terms of battling outside the ring – this would soon change. Some friends of ours were having a row with another teenage gang. We weren't too concerned as they seemed evenly matched, but then the other gang started using their feet. One of our friends went down and three pairs of boots were kicking him from head to toe. This escalation from what we considered fair, into foul, happened in seconds. It goes without saying that Ron and I joined in pretty quick and, although against our principles, 'put the boot in'.

Talking about the incident as we were getting ready for bed that night I found that Ron had felt the same way as I did when we witnessed the brawl. That it was disgusting and cowardly that anyone could consider using their feet in a fight. But this was to be another turning point in our lives, for we both decided then that if the rules had changed then we would change with them, but with an extra vow. If that's what it took to come out on top then we would kick harder and better than any of our adversaries. We had embraced some street-fighting philosophy: Do as you would be done by – but do it first and with more force. Or all is fair in war. Strangely enough, this new-found taste for fighting and giving violence to those who asked for it never affected our boxing. We kept the two styles separate and in the ring stuck by the rules.

One day brother Charlie took us to the Rupert Browning

Institute near Elephant and Castle. To be able to join you had to prove yourself capable of handling yourself. So, like an audition, we had to do a few rounds with one of the members. According to Charlie, the trainers who watched us were well impressed and wanted us to join straight away. Before we went back to the club the next time, Charlie generously took us to a sports shop in Ludgate Circus. The memory of that shop stays with me until this day. The clean smell of new leather and waxes and the exciting equipment mesmerised my young eyes. Weights, punchbags, medicine balls, but best of all was the section with footwear because our brother was buying us a brand-new pair of black leather boxing boots. We were so proud of these prized possessions we couldn't wait to get home so we could show our parents.

Our trainer at the Rupert Browning Institute was an ex-pro by the name of Charlie Simms. With his broken nose, scar tissue over both eyes, and two oddly shaped cauliflower ears, his looks were a contradiction of the fact that he was or had been an excellent defensive fighter. He taught us a lot and in no time we were getting mentions in the *East London Advertiser*. In a safe place outside the prison, I have four thick scrapbooks containing cuttings referring to Ron and myself from the age of twelve. It's been many years since I last looked through these books, but I know that if they were brought in to me today and I were to flick through the yellowed cuttings of our short boxing career, the same pride and excitement I felt then would come flooding back.

As I sat at the kitchen table with scissors and paste in the 1940s I could not have imagined the pieces I carefully cut from the local sports pages would one day be dwarfed by an avalanche of newsprint as we became infamous in the eyes of the media. Starting off with a win in the Hackney Area Championships, I followed this with a unanimous verdict in the prestigious London Schoolboy Boxing Championships. This win made me very proud and I could see my dreams of becoming World Champion getting closer and closer. From there I went on to fight in the Great Britain Schoolboy Championships; which meant a trip to Leeds where the fight was to be held. I put everything I had into that boxing match. I was confident, I kept my cool, put up a good defence, and as I attacked my opponent in flurries of good punches the points were clocking up in my head as if on a taxi metre. But at the final bell, the other boy's hand was held up as the winner on points and I felt gutted. I was sportsman enough to take a beating and it wasn't the first fight I'd lost but this time I knew in my heart the title should have gone to me. I blamed the decision on those northern judges who were biased against London boxers. This wasn't just my personal opinion; even people from the local area told me they thought the judges were out of order.

As an amateur boxer I lost a total of five matches out of fifty-five, and as a professional won seven out of seven. I got as far as the Great Britain Semi-Final at Wembley Arena, but on the day could not make the weight, so had to miss the fight. In one of these competitions I had three fights in one night. In the first bout I won in the first round, the second in the second round, and won the third on points.

Ron's record was very similar to my own and he had equal success. In the London Schoolboy Boxing Championships we had both reached the finals three years running. Because our talents were equal, although our styles were completely different, we had seen off the competition so well that one day we faced each other in the ring. As twins we were mentally closer than ordinary brothers, yet when the bell went for the start of three two-minute rounds we were strangers and got stuck into each other like tigers. By the second round we were both bleeding – me from his slugging, almost cobble-fighter's attack, and him from my more boxing-like punches. Just before the third round I glanced ringside and saw Mum with her hands over her face and Dad and Charlie frowning. I could tell none of them were enjoying the spectacle. The final round was bloodier still, because neither of us would give the other an inch. We were evenly matched and giving equal punishment. In the end I got the verdict, though it must have been as close as you could get. Afterwards Mum laid into both of us for hurting each other the way we had, but I think this was her way of letting out the fear she had felt while watching us. She told us that a couple of times she got out of her seat to stop us but Dad had stopped her.

Another time Ron and I fought at a fairground, but Mum wasn't there and it wasn't half as bloody. Ron and I went to a fun fair that had been set up on a bomb-site in Turin Road off Bethnal Green Road. We wandered among colourful rides to a background of loud organ music, tried our hands on the coconut shies and rifle range, until at the far end we came across a boxing booth. This was set up in a marquee and out front was a wooden stage painted all round with figures of fighters. On the stage stood Alf Stuart throwing out challenges to the public plus a lot of showman's banter to whip the crowd up and encourage them to take on one of his fighters.

These fighters, all ex-boxers and well past their prime, would stand behind Alf as he introduced them by name: Slasher Warner, Les Haycock, Johnny Cunningham and the Osbourne brothers, Steve and Buster. Each of these men looked like the stereotypical boxer who has passed his prime. Their circumstances were terrible too, as purses were not like they are today. Prize money for some of the best crowd pullers might only have been three hundred pounds, which even translated to today's terms was no fortune. When the limelight had faded most of them ended up as tappers – which meant they were skint and spent the rest of their lives tapping others for a drink or a couple of shillings. The alternative was to tour the booths as these men did, taking and handing out punishment for a pound a round. Though they were big men with formidable looks – lumpy hands, broken noses and faces lined with scar tissue – often they were in their sixties and no matter how seasoned they were, facing tough dockers or draymen in their twenties perhaps ten times in a night must have been hard to keep up with.

Still, this attraction was right up our street, so we handed over our money and entered the booth. The smell of the place was unforgettable. Blood, sweat, leather and the pungent odour of wintergreen liniment. The atmosphere was charged with excitement too, as under a pall of cigarette smoke and the glare of arc lights the crowd shuffled in anticipation. With a full house Alf would close the canvas doors, jump in the ring and go into his spiel for challengers. Most of his patter would be directed at likely lads around the ringside. His experience in crowd psychology would tell him that a direct challenge to an onlooker would be hard to turn down in front of his mates. 'Keep on your feet for three short rounds with one of my boys and I'll give you five pounds. One hundred shiny shillings – now how bad can that be?' That was well over a week's wages for the average working man. Once a combatant had climbed into the ring, one of the booth fighters would follow him. This first time it was Slasher, but before the bell went Alf made a tongue-in-cheek apology: 'Now remember, if Mr Warner here infringes the rules you must not judge him too harshly because as a street-fighter and bookie's bodyguard, he's never heard of Queensberry rules.' That got a laugh from the crowd. The first young bloke lasted almost to the end of round one and I'm sure the timekeeper held off ringing the bell until Slasher had finished kicking the fella in the ribs as he lay on the floor.

Some of the crowd booed but most screamed in delight. This is what they'd paid to see and so it went on, fight after fight. Ron and I loved it.

Then Alf said, 'Right, now for something different. If any of you lot want to settle a difference or have a bit of fun, get up in this ring, fight it out and I'll see you all right.' Ron and I looked at each other and didn't have to say a word. We just put our hands up and climbed into the ring. They gloved me up and sorted us out. A big cheer erupted from the crowd when Alf introduced us as, 'These up-and-coming twins, Reg and Ron Kray, are going to give an exhibition of how it should be done.' Once again we went at each other hammer and tongs and gave the punters their money's worth. Ron's nose was bleeding and I had a vivid bruise on my cheekbone, and we were so carried away our faces were bright red. Because it was just a bit of entertainment, there was no winner or loser. But if points had been given I think a draw could have been the only result. Alf gave us seven shillings and sixpence each, patted us on the shoulders and said, 'Anytime you boys want to put on a show again I'll find a slot for you.' We ran home and handed the money over to Mum, having made sure we had cleaned off the blood and tidied ourselves up in case she got upset again.

When I was telling Uncle Joe about it he said, 'I remember on of those blokes when they were a bit younger. They were in the booth then and very popular with the crowd. But a little scam they worked was that the MC would come out and say, "Ladies and Gentlemen, bit of bad news – somebody's stolen one of the fighter's wallets and left him with nothing." Straight away the hat would go round a sympathetic crowd and the take would be split between the fighters. It was only done every now and again but it never failed.'

Many years later I was walking along the Roman Road and a shuffling grey-haired old man was unsteadily making his way towards me. What caught my attention was his distinctive turned-up nose that had obviously been broken a few times. Just at the moment I recognised him as Slasher Warner, he turned into the local doss house, a place where down and outs could get a bed for a few shillings. What I was thinking of at that time I don't know, but the fact that I didn't follow him and give him a few quid to help out has remained one of the many regrets of my life. I never saw him again, which was a great shame as he was a colourful character who deserved better in his last days.

I know I haven't had the pleasure of walking the streets of the East End for over a quarter of a century but I still know what goes on, and from what I hear characters of the type that punctuated my childhood and youth no longer exist. Different times breed different people, I suppose. One of the men we looked up to was Jimmy Spinks, an old-time fighter who epitomised the tough East Ender. Known as the Guv'nor of Hoxton, at five feet nine inches tall, shoulders like an ox, large hands and powerful neck, he looked formidable and he was.

His reputation as a fighter was renowned as well as the fact that no matter how many he was up against in defence or attack, the only 'tools' he used were his bare fists. His face was a road map of knife or razor cuts that bore testimony to the fact that no one dared face him without a weapon. Years later I would become friends with his nephew, the equally formidable Lenny 'The Guv'nor' McLean. There were so many similarities between the two it was almost like reincarnation.

By the time we got to know Jimmy Spinks, his fighting days were behind him and he was content to sit outside the Spread Eagle public house in Shoreditch with sleeves rolled up and held in place by old-fashioned armbands around his huge biceps. As kids, Ron and I would often sit with him and listen to his stories and he'd buy us lemonade or take us to the sweet shop next door and treat us to a handful of silver-foil-wrapped chocolate coins.

Wassle was another character we'd see outside the pub more often than not: thick-set, barrel-chested and dressed immaculately. In his career as a villain he didn't give a fuck for anyone and would return any slight upset or violence tenfold. One lunchtime in the local pub he got into an argument with the boxer Alby Day, a contender who fought in the stable of Jack Solomons. It didn't come to blows, but later as Wassle was relieving himself in the toilet, Alby crept in, caught him unawares, and with a crafty right-hander knocked him to the floor. Thinking he'd had the last word Alby went back to the bar and resumed his drinking. Ten minutes later he had a chain coiled around his neck and found himself being dragged from the pub like a dog. Wassle had recovered, gone through a side door and taken the heavy chain from a cart outside. Once Alby was on the pavement he soon learned the difference between fighting in the ring and fighting in the street.

On another occasion Wassle politely suggested to the owner of a local fish and chip shop that a weekly pension for himself might help in keeping the shop in one piece. Equally politely, the shop keeper declined the offer, so without further argument Wassle reached into the window where a cat was sunning itself, grabbed the animal by the neck and threw it into the fish fryer. He got his payment.

These, and many other respected villains of the day, we got to know through our father. Although he wasn't a villain himself or a fighting man in the same sense as they were, Dad spent a lot of time in their company. Not that he couldn't have a scrap if the situation arose – with a drink inside him he could be a right handful. One night him and Aunt Rose's husband Billy Wiltshire went out for a drink together, got into an argument with some other blokes and finished up hammering the lot of them. At that time my parents lived in a couple of upstairs rooms in a house, while Uncle Joe occupied one of the lower rooms. Three o'clock in the morning a copper from Old Street nick came banging on the door. He wants to know that as they've got the old man and Bill locked up would Joe like to come and bail them out? Because he had the hump at being dragged out of bed in the early hours Joe said, 'No I won't – fucking well keep 'em for a week,' and shut the door. Mum didn't know anything about it until the old man came home the following afternoon with the raging hump at Uncle Joe.

It's not surprising that Ron and I learned to settle differences with others by resorting to violence – we were surrounded by it. If I described every fight one or the other of the family got into, these stories would fill a book on their own. I could imagine that in other areas where society was different a fight of any description would be a shocking thing, something to talk about for weeks, but where we came from it was common enough to be hardly worth noting. I can remember Grandad Lee having a row with a neighbour, George Connor, who lived on the corner. At first it was just angry words, and then Grandad swung a right, caught George squarely on the chin and knocked him sprawling in the street. If Uncle John hadn't come along and physically carried Grandad away, God knows what further damage he would have inflicted.

Even family was not allowed to get away with liberty-taking. Grandad had an argument with his brother Tom, but it seemed to be settled and he forgot about it. He'd been out for a bicycle ride and was just leaning the bike against the wall when up the road came Uncle Tom. As he came past a neighbour shouted, 'Look out Jimmy, this fella's got a lump of iron behind his back.' Uncle Tom was going to attack his own brother with an iron bar. I suppose it was the weapon that upset Grandad most. He ran to meet Tom, grabbed the bar and flung it up the street, then set about him until he was unconscious in the gutter. It took four blokes to hold Grandad back, otherwise he might have killed his own brother. No law got involved but they didn't speak to each other for many years afterwards.

This Uncle Tom, or I should say great uncle, was a bit of a character in his own right, and according to family stories was a bit slippery. In his younger days he lived near and was friendly with the Bristol bantamweight boxer, Pedlar Palmer. Pedlar had had a crack at the world title but he was knocked out by Terry McGovern in what was then the briefest title fight in ring history. Somebody gave Uncle Tom half a dozen expensive silk shirts to pass on to the boxer, but after weighing up the risks against a few quid in his own pocket, he decided that Pedlar with all his money wouldn't need a few extra shirts, so he sold them off. As often happened in the close-knit community of the East End, word got back to the boxer and Uncle Tom had to keep his head down for a long time as the threat was made that he would be put down the sink by Pedlar and his mob.

Another time he wasn't so clever either. He was working as a foreman at Pool Wharf with half a dozen men under him when he was approached by a very smartly dressed man. The man explained that he leased one of the buildings on the wharf but unfortunately had lost the key. Trouble was it was urgent for him to remove some goods he had in storage. At the same time he made it clear that once the door was unlocked he would be looking to hire some men for a few hours to help with the loading – said men to be well looked after. Uncle Tom, who could never turn down the chance of a few extra bob, nearly fell over in his haste to help the man. By the time the man returned with a large van, Tom had made himself busy. The padlock was smashed off and the workers were standing by the door ready to go to work. While the man sorted the furs that the warehouse contained, the six men under Tom's orders formed a chain and loaded the van until it couldn't hold any more. All finished, a new padlock was fixed to the door and lining the men up the fur trader thanked them, shook their hands and gave each of them ten shillings, with an extra half-crown for Uncle Tom. They must have cheered him off the dock because ten bob was a lot of money then. As you might have already guessed, two days later the real owner turned up. He had to force the new padlock, then called the police. An inspector collared Tom and asked him if he'd seen anyone suspicious loading up stolen furs. Tom replied, 'Yes Guv'nor – a big guy and we all helped him.'

Even the female side of the family inherited the fighting genes. Not so much Mum or Auntie May, though they did have a scrap one day between themselves and May ended up with a black eye, but they were young and it was a one-off. But Auntie Rose was a fighter all her life. I loved them all, but Rose was my favourite. With her long black hair, green eyes and fiery temper she was like an attractive gypsy, and Ron and I spent hours in her company. You could bet if we were not indoors at home we'd be next door drinking tea and eating biscuits with her, listening to her stories and discussing all kind of topics. If she had half a crown she'd give away two bob to anyone who needed it, just like our mother. But that temper of hers! Luckily we were never at the receiving end of it because she'd loved us since we were babies, but we often saw her lay into others. We'd be sitting in her front room and she'd say, 'See them nosey bastards Mr and Mrs So-and-so down the road, next time they give me one of their looks I'm going to spit in their eyes' – and she meant it. Other times, if she saw a copper walking up the road, she'd wait until he was about to pass her door then, as though it was an accident, she'd shake a dusty rug in his face.

Uncle Joe and her were in a beer house one night in the days when public houses needed a proper licence to sell strong spirits. After a while their mother, Nanny Lee, came in with a friend of hers, went up to the bar and ordered two tots of whisky. The barman explained he couldn't sell spirits, but she wouldn't listen and kicked up a row. Her language, as usual, could make a docker blush, 'Fuckin' bastard, if you won't serve us you can fuck off – we'll go somewhere else.' Then Nan and her mate stormed out. The pub was packed and on their way out they barged into a couple of blokes. One of them said, 'Oi, you mind who your fuckinwell shoving.' Joe's not having his mother spoken to like that so he pushes through the crowd to have a go at the two blokes. As they are about to set about Joe, Rose sees it and joins in. But she doesn't go through the crush, she goes over it. She jumped on the bar and then ran over heads and shoulders screaming, 'Leave my brother alone.' When she reached them she squared up and punched like a man. The blokes couldn't get out of her way quick enough.

But God help anyone who touched Rose's son Billy. On one occasion when he was threatened she pulled a knife on the other person. As I said, before he went in the army Billy was the scourge of everybody. For some reason or other he'd upset Billy and Alfie Kray. Whatever he'd said or done must have been serious because word came back that they were going to give him a good hiding. This time it was Nanny Lee who jumped to his defence. Billy and Alfie each had a stall selling second-hand clothes down the market, so on the Sunday morning Nan's down there screaming at them like a mad woman. She must have been seventy-five then but she certainly put the wind up my two uncles. 'What's this about you going to do my Billy up? Well, I'll tell you two Krays, any of you mob lay a finger on him I'll come back and turn these fucking stalls over.'

Sadly Aunt Rose was diagnosed with leukaemia but even that didn't dampen her fighting spirit. She'd been having treatment for the disease, been away for convalescence and had just come home when she got a visit from a couple of friends of hers, Jimmy Stannard and his sister – both well pissed. A row had developed and the sister had got stuck into Rose, who being under the weather at the time couldn't do much to retaliate. A couple of weeks later, Mum and Rose were walking down Bethnal Green Road. As they got to the butcher's on the corner along came the woman Stannard. Outside the shop were trays and trays of eggs, all displayed on the slant. Mum tried to steer Rose away but all she said was, 'Keep out of it Violi, now it's my turn.' She pushed up her sleeves and punched the woman three or four times, leaving her sprawled among hundreds of broken eggs. She said to the bloke who owned the shop, an ex-boxer with huge cauliflower ears, 'Get her to pay for the eggs, she broke 'em.' He never said a word.

Shortly after this incident, our beautiful Aunt Rose died in the London Hospital. Despite being the generous and wonderfully outgoing person she was, inside she was an emotional and lonely woman – even though she was surrounded by family who loved her. We were all devastated to lose her.

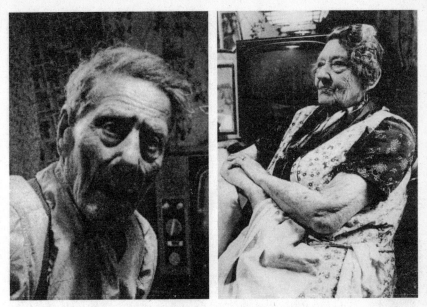

Grandad and Grandma Lee – East End legends in their own right.

Dad's business card. He didn't let anything get in the way of his role as breadwinner – not even conscription.

My wonderful parents.

A young Ron and me (either side of the trophy) posing with the boxing club.

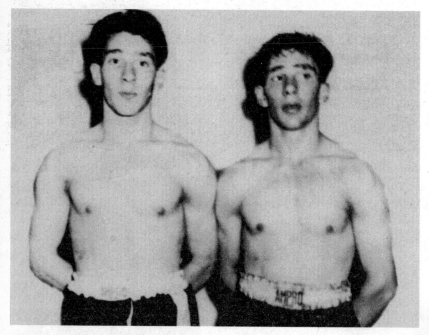

A few years later before a fight.

'Kray Vs Kray' – as close as we were outside the ring, inside it we were vicious.

Fruit-picking in Wisbech with Mum (top left), Ron (centre) and the family. One of my fondest memories.

Rex might have looked fierce but he was as soft as they come.

My favourite aunt, Rose, and me on Lee Corner, or Vallance Road as it was officially known.

Outside the house with Mum. In the distance you can see the railway line German bombs targeted during the war.

Regal Motors, on Eric Street, formed part of our first place of business.

Brother Charlie (right), some associates and me at The Regal Billiard Hall. From here our empire grew further than we'd ever imagined.

My beloved Frances and me surrounded by our families on our wedding day in 1965.

Frances was my greatest joy in life – we had many happy times together and this is a reminder of one of them.

Reggie Kray 1933–2000.

5

Getting into Business

As a boy, something I got great pleasure from was visiting my grandfather Jimmy Kray. Gorsuch Street, where he lived, was a turning off Hackney Road and no more than a five-minute walk away from our house. Usually the front door would be wedged open with a large round stone that was so smooth and shiny I can only imagine that he had found it by the sea at some time. If the door was shut, all I had to do was pull a piece of string and it would release the latch. In the passageway an enormous aspidistra plant would seem to reach out and snag my jersey as I walked by. In the front room where Farvie would be sitting in a large comfortable armchair, the most dominant thing was a highly polished walnut piano.

At this time, Farvie, like Grandad Lee, would have been in his seventies and still as tough as they come. We'd have a cup of tea and a few digestive biscuits and he'd comment on different bits of news from the paper on his knee. Then he'd turn to the sports page and ask me what I thought of Don Cockell's chances against Rocky Marciano, and would I be staying up to listen to the fight on the wireless, which was being broadcast from San Francisco in the early hours of the morning. That would set him off on a train of conversation that I loved. Joe Louis, Max Baer, Primo Carnera, Jack Dempsey – gradually he'd get further and further back in time as he spoke of this fight and that fight, until he'd be back in the days of Bob Fitzsimmons, James Corbett and Jem Smith – heroes of his own youth. I'd sit there fascinated as he described boxers who to me were straight from the history books.

It wasn't just stories of his old boxing heroes that Farvie would talk about – he loved to reminisce about his own youth. I was up in his bedroom one day and I noticed an iron bar sticking out from behind the pillows on his bed. When I asked him what it was there for he said, 'Just in case someone tries to pull a caper like they did with Nosher.' Old Nosher Powell, father of the stunt man and referee, wasn't short of money and had a tendency to flash it about. One night he hung his trousers on the end of the bed with £200 in the back pocket. This cash, a fortune in those days, must have been noticed when he was in the pub earlier in the evening. Later, someone with a lot of nerve, considering Nosher's reputation, got a ladder, climbed into his bedroom, and pinched the money and the trousers. The next day he accused his best mate Sonny of robbing him and punched him a couple of times. Sonny, who was also a tough old boy, picked up a lump of wood and knocked Nosher unconscious.

I loved hearing Grandad Kray's stories so I was over the moon every time he asked me to help him with his second-hand clothes business, in the hope of hearing another. I'd be sent up to Shoreditch on a Sunday morning to collect a barrow from a man who hired them out. I'd have to wait while the elderly white-haired man, who had a club foot, slowly undid the chain that ran through the wheels of a line of barrows. Back at Grandad's house in Gorsuch Street I'd run up and down the stairs fetching and loading up black cloth bags from the back room that were filled with the gear that he'd bought on his travels. With the barrow piled high I'd run with it all the way to Brick Lane, using the effort as extra training for my legs, chest and general stamina. Once I got the barrow parked at our usual pitch outside a shoe shop, it would be my job to set out the clothes ready for sale. You name it, we had it. Shoes, suits, shirts, waistcoats, overcoats and ex-army greatcoats. All good quality and in high demand by the punters. When Grandad went off for a tea break he'd leave me in charge and I'd enjoy the haggling, bartering and banter that was part of the fun of market trading. If business was brisk while he was gone, I'd feel proud to hand over a pile of ten-bob notes, half-crowns and shillings. When there were slack periods I would take an idea I'd picked up from a film on the life of the great fighter Jim Corbett. Mingling among the densely packed crowd, I'd swerve and side-step around the people in the market without touching them, which I found was an interesting way of improving my footwork and sense of balance. Working with Grandad was a lot of fun and I never expected or looked for any reward, but at the end of the day he would always insist on giving me seven shillings and sixpence, which for a lad of thirteen was very good money.

Though I spent a lot of time with Farvie, I suppose because he was just over the back, I spent more with Grandad Lee. I'd always be in and out to see what he was up to next, because although he wasn't an educated man, he had a wonderful talent with his hands. He was always bringing broken instruments back from the market, which he'd picked up for a couple of shillings, and a hour or two after he got them home he'd be knocking a tune out, whether it was a violin, banjo or an accordion. He even built a car in the upstairs bedroom of his house, but had to dismantle it to get it outside. He had green fingers too, and one year received first prize in a competition run by the local council for best window-box display. Two nights later he threw every flowerpot down into the street, at a load of yobboes making a racket.

*

As a family one of the things we looked forward to the most was the annual fruit-picking holiday. This traditional exodus to the fields and orchards of Kent, Surrey, Cambridge and many other parts of the country, had been made by Londoners for generation after generation. Long before the season started, advertisements would appear in the local press inviting families to apply for work. As everyone from grandparents down to sturdy five-year-olds could add some contribution to the collective effort good money could be earned, so naturally they jumped at the chance to get away from the grimy streets of the East End. And although the work was hard and the hours long, the six to eight weeks spent in a rural environment was the highlight of the year.

Our first working trip was to a farm in the fens of Cambridge near the town of Wisbech. Ron, our parents and I were accommodated in long wooden army-type huts, along with all the other workers, in a field near the farmhouse. Inside, they were partitioned off with plasterboard walls to give each family some privacy. It wasn't long before Ron and I started to need some entertainment, so to keep ourselves occupied we got the gloves on. We got stuck into each other and getting a bit carried away, we ended up splitting some of the panels as we crashed each other into them. That got us a telling off from Mum, so we stuck to sparring outside after that.

The work of picking strawberries was back-breaking and monotonous, but we loved being out in the fresh air. With the younger workers there was a certain amount of friendly rivalry going on as to who could fill the most baskets. We were only paid for the amount we picked, so these races helped us towards a good pay-out at the end of the day. If I remember correctly, each filled punnet was worth about ninepence, so collectively our family could pick up eight or nine pounds for a week's work on the Saturday night.

Sometimes we would be put onto gooseberry picking, which was not half as back-breaking, but could be painful if your leather gloves were left in the hut. The following year we turned up with our parents and a friend, Pat Butler, to find there was no room in the huts for us boys, so that evening in the pub Mum approached the gangmaster Bill Shippey and asked him what we could do. Without hesitation he said the three of us could move into his home for the season, which began a friendship with Bill and his wife Mavis that has lasted to the present day.

Any reader who imagines that because of our reputation the Kray twins ran riot and generally terrorised the people of Wisbech would be surprised to hear how Bill's wife described us. On a recent visit to me here at Maidstone, Mavis, who for some reason I've always called Mary, told me that Ron and I had been quiet, considerate and polite. She also reminded me of how we would always insist on clearing the table after our meals, or were for ever offering to make her cups of tea. I learned too with great pleasure that one of Bill's most treasured possessions is a wooden musical box in the shape of a house that Ron and I made between us and sent to them in the very early years of our prison sentence.

One incident that happened while we were there literally left its mark. Ron, Pat and I went camping nearby on our Sunday off. Everything went great until darkness fell. As one of us lit a candle for a bit of light the whole tent went up in flames. In the panic I scrambled out, fell against a barbed-wire fence and severely lacerated my back. It was incredibly painful and I still bear the scars. Years later, when I was sent to prison for GBH, this incident came back to mind. One of the first things that happens once you are behind the door is a medical examination. After the indignity of having my testicles cupped by the doctor while being told to cough, and the even worse indignity of him rooting through my pubic hair for lice or crabs, he asked me to turn round. He was quiet for a moment, then touching the scars from the barbed wire, he enquired, 'Ever been flogged, Kray?' I replied, 'No sir'. His sneering reply was, 'It's a great pity.'

Back in the East End, like all kids, the end of our childhood was signalled by starting work for a living, full time. Apart from working towards being boxing World Champion, neither of us had any ambition as far as a career, so we were prepared to tackle anything that would bring in a few quid.

Uncle Joe fixed up our first job. He was working down Billingsgate fish market and one of the governors asked him if he knew of a boy who'd be willing to do the running around. Joe said, 'Well, I do as it happens, but it's not one boy, it's two – they're my twin nephews and look so much alike I can't tell the difference, so I wouldn't know which one to ask.' The boss said he could find work for the both of us. So Ron was taken on in the haddock market as 'empty boy' for the firm Farren & Barrow, where his job was to collect empty fish boxes, while I was sent to the shop in Thames Street as a junior salesman, supposedly to learn the business of selling to customers. I hadn't been there long when, after making up a large parcel of fish for a man, he said, 'Do me a favour son. Will you take it and put it in my motor. The cart minder will tell you which one it is, and I'll have to see you later because I've no change on me.' I did as he asked and thought no more of it. The following week he came back again and asked me to deliver another order. He was a customer, so I had to be polite, but I wasn't going to be done. I said, 'You promised you'd see me all right the last time I ran an errand for you but you haven't come across.' He gave me a strange look as though I wasn't all there and said, 'What's up with you? I squared up the day after when I saw you down the market.' Then the penny dropped – he'd seen Ron and paid out, thinking he was me. When I caught up with my brother, I asked him if some bloke had given him money and he said, 'Yes, half a crown.' When I said it was mine and wanted it he told me to fuck off, so that was the end of that. I was a bit put out at the time, but I could see the humour in it.

I'd always loved the atmosphere of Billingsgate Market and even as a little kid wanted to work there one day. The toing and froing and the bustle and hurry-up of the porters as they raced around pushing barrows laden with boxes of fish, or else wearing large leather hats on which they'd balance a number of boxes on their head. They called this 'nutting the fish'. The air was always full of noise: shouts of the men mingled with the shrieks and cries of the gulls as they swept in from the nearby Thames, snatched a fish, then steered away with a haunting squawk of triumph. The smells, the clutter and the camaraderie of the people who worked there gave a zest to the day that I find difficult to convey to those who have never experienced it. But it was also a mysterious place. Early one morning, long before I started travelling to market with him, Uncle Joe had been driving his cart along when he noticed that the surface of the road ahead seemed to be moving. At first he thought his eyes were playing up, but as he reigned in the horses and slowed down, thousands upon thousands of rats converged on him. They covered the full width of the road and as far as he could see in front of him. What he found unnerving was their sense of purpose and utter silence as they surged around the wheels and hooves of the horses. Eventually they passed him, but even today he has never understood what the phenomenon signified.

This strange and exciting place was so enticing to me as a teenager that I'd be waiting outside the front door listening for the sound of Uncle Joe's horse and cart approaching, even though it might be as early as 3 a.m. in the morning. Good-looking, well-built and six foot three, my uncle was an imposing figure. I used to feel quite proud sitting up in the cart with him as we glided through the cobbled streets. Sometimes he'd be driving a double-horse cart but other times, depending on the load, he might have four sturdy animals in the shafts. Although I was just starting my day's work, he had already been to one of the stations and picked up boxes of mackerel, herring or skate. The novelty would wear off in time, but in the early weeks I'd sit high up behind the steaming horses and imagine I was one of the American settlers heading into the West on my stagecoach.

When we arrived at the market, the first thing we'd have to do would be to get the cart safely parked up and left for unloading. The second thing – and the best – was to head for the little café on the hill for cheese rolls or dripping on toast with big mugs of tea. Either inside the café or passing the window we'd often see famous old boxers from the past, who, now that their glory had passed them by, were trying to earn a living. And though we didn't know it at the time, we'd also see famous names yet to come. Two such soon to be famous men were George and Billy Walker. George fought for the title of Light Heavyweight Champion of Great Britain against Freddie Powell of Wales. His brother Billy was as game as they come and had many great fights in the heavyweight class. Unfortunately the British title he aimed for always eluded him, but in later years he turned his hand to acting and was very successful.

After a few months down the market I started getting restless. I still enjoyed the work but felt like a change, so Ron and I turned it in and began looking around for what would be the second in a long line of short-lived casual jobs. We got fixed up in the area of Bow Canal as labourers and found the hard physical labour suited us both. It wasn't long before our fitness and stamina reached a new peak and due to the fact that we spent day after day breaking rocks with sledgehammers, our muscles turned to iron – a great asset in tackling the aggravation that was slowly creeping into our lives. Violence was never to be far away.

One day, a fella at work called Ginger Davey got a bit mouthy with Ron. Being a few years older and being more experienced in the work we were doing must have given him the idea he could take the piss, but looking at Ron's face I could see the bloke had made a big mistake. He threw a couple of words at Ron, then with a smirk on his face climbed up a long ramp and carried on working under a lean-to shed. I knew it wasn't finished, so as I was working I kept an eye on Ron. Sure enough, ten minutes later I saw him creep up the ramp, pick up a lump of rock and smash Davey over the head with it. Down he went. I ran up the ramp and fortunately got to the shed quick enough to grapple with my brother and talk him out of inflicting more injury with the rock. Davey was stunned and bleeding profusely but with his bottle completely gone I was able to pacify the situation without further repercussions. For the rest of our short stay in that job he made sure he kept as far away from us as possible.

We soon moved on. Still by the canal, in an area of Queensbury Road, but this time we worked on a casual basis under the direction of ganger Big Tommy Cheshire, a very large man, well known for being more than capable of looking after himself. Again this work was physically demanding as we were unloading long, heavy planks of wood from barges to the quayside. With leather shoulder pads as protection against chafing and grazes, we'd walk up and down the gangplank all day like robots. In the end the boring monotony of the work and the lousy wages became too much to bear, so it was off to Truman's Brewery.

As far as work went, the only difference was a change of scenery, because endlessly stacking crates of beer turned out to be equally boring. It had its perks, though. Officially we were allowed a couple of pints of brown or light ale a day. Needless to say, the official quota was totally ignored, which helped the hours pass in a pleasant daze.

Larceny at work was part of life and a short spell in the tin factory at the back of Hackney Road supplied family and neighbours with enough kettles to last a lifetime. But as far as earning decent money from this bit of thieving went, there was a limit to how many kettles and tea pots could be smuggled out. But when I joined a firm of scent-makers in

Bishopsgate, I hit a little goldmine. The size of the product allowed me to walk through the gates with a tidy sum in the form of contraband hidden in every pocket and even stuck down my pants. At Christmas time I could hardly keep up with the orders from stallholders who didn't question where the goods were coming from. Better still was Joyce's Lingerie down Old Street in Shoreditch. This firm sold ladies' underwear wholesale. At first I was in the packing department, making up parcels for dispatch. Once I got the hang of a bit of sleight of hand, most of the parcels were going out a bit light. Eventually I was earning more from nicking than I was being paid in wages. Soon an opportunity arose to earn some real money. I was asked to take over the job of driver's mate on the delivery lorry. The driver was an easy-going fella in his forties, who, like everyone else, was struggling to make a living on piss-poor wages. So when I suggested we divert the load for our own ends, he jumped at the idea. The safest way to approach the theft was to drive straight to a lock-up owned by a relation of mine and unload the gear. Once that was done all we had to do was leave the lorry in the car park of a transport café and go for a meal. An hour later, go out to the lorry and then run back inside shouting that some bastard has nicked our load. We deserved Oscars. I think the Old Bill had a fair idea of what had gone down but they had nothing to go on and had to accept our story. My relation squared us up and I cut it sixty-forty in my favour with the driver. After all it was my idea and nobody was hurt except the insurance company. I was quite proud of how I handled this step up from petty theft, but was not aware that a scam of this nature would pale into insignificance against what I would undertake in the future.

Life wasn't all about work. In our spare time we'd hang about with lads of our own age in what could loosely be called a gang. One of the places we enjoyed frequenting was a local theatre, the Hackney Empire. The names of those who performed on the bill will mean nothing to young people today, but they were some of the greatest names in the business. George Formby and his ukulele, Issy Brown, the Jewish singer, and the hilarious Arthur Lucan who dressed up as Old Mother Riley and did an act with Kitty, who was supposed to be her daughter onstage but was in fact his wife. We'd watch these acts from way up in the gods, which is what the cheapest seats in the upper balconies were known as, but at the same time we'd be scanning the theatre for rivals, for being young bloods there was always friction with other gangs as each juggled for the position of superiority.

One night I spotted a young gang leader by the name of Lamb. For some time this fella had been shooting his mouth off about what he'd do if he got hold of me. I wasn't that hard to find if he was so keen to mix it, as he said he was, but he'd never sought me out. Now it would be the other way round. I kept my eyes on him and when he went to the toilets, I slipped out of my seat and followed him. As I walked in and shut the door behind me he looked round and I struck him across the face with a length of bicycle chain. His nose and mouth burst open and he fell down amongst the piss and dog-ends screaming his head off. I calmly pocketed the chain, joined the others and we left the theatre, leaving behind another brick for the wall of reputation that was building around us as young villains.

We had well-earned reputations as boxers, which had been established since we were twelve. But over a period of time we found we were gaining a certain notoriety due to our street-fighting prowess. In a way we were forced to perpetuate the growing myth, as certain individuals and many gangs sought us out in their efforts to enhance their own reputations as those who had sorted out those Kray Twins. We had fights wherever we went, and in consequence found we were barred from dance halls and cinemas all over the East End and north London. I remember going to the Rex Cinema in Bethnal Green. The manager, done up in his penguin suit, was standing just inside the foyer vetting the customers. When he saw us he said, 'I don't want you lot in here causing trouble,' so Ron hit him full on the chin and sent him sprawling. Though we didn't intentionally look for trouble it seemed to come looking for us. Invariably the odds seemed stacked against us, but without false modesty I can honestly say that when Ron and myself were shoulder to shoulder we were a match for half a dozen of our opponents.

On one such occasion we were in the Coach and Horses with our friend Pat Butler, the fella that used to go to

Wisbech with us, when we were ready-eyed by a nine-handed little mob at the other end of the pub. Pat is no fighter and I knew something was coming up so I told him to fuck off quick. I had a quick word with Ron, then ran out of the door as though I was scared, leaving him behind. Just as I'd guessed, half of them came charging after me. I ran up the road, dodged down a couple of alleyways and came back into the pub just in time to see Ron smash a chair over the head of one of the young blokes. There was five of them, one down, two each left. Ron in front, me behind – they'd nowhere to go except on the floor and we'd just put them there when the other four burst back in. Tables went over, glasses were smashed, but between us we hammered the lot of them. There was blood everywhere – none of ours and most of it from the bloke who'd been done with the chair, but they'd started it so we just walked away and never gave them another thought.

Caught unawares, we weren't tooled up that night, but normally if we felt we were going into a potentially violent situation we'd sort out something from under our bed in Vallance Road. The collection of weapons we had was large enough to cope with anything short of a war. Before we went to a dance or whatever, we'd tell the rest of the gang to come up to the bedroom and sort something out for themselves. The choice included knuckle-dusters, bowie knives, coshes, Ghurka knives, cut-throat razors, and – even sharper than razors – a surgeon's scalpel. If we needed to improvise, a lethal and not too obvious cosh could be made by putting a spanner inside a tie, knotting the bottom, and then tucking it into the trousers. More than once I went out with a sword down my trousers. Walking with a slight limp was no problem, but being unable to bend my leg getting on the bus to go to the Royal in Tottenham was very awkward.

Every area had its own gang, and where there were leaders like John Nash, Ronnie Diamond and Tony Pachita there would be followers aligning themselves with ferocious loyalty under the banner of the leader's name. We had no quarrel with the Nash gang, in fact we were quite friendly with them. Even today I class John as a good friend. With some of the others we had an uneasy truce. In the main, confrontation with most meant an explosion of violence. A dice game in the toilet area of Shoreditch Town Hall ended in a battle when we found some cheating was going on. Our gang pulled out concealed weapons and done the lot of them. The same happened when we got into a row with Tony Pachita and his gang at a north London coffee stall. He was part-Italian and a bit flash, but once we'd gone through the lot of them they weren't feeling so clever.

Our reputation was so great that even when we were on our own, the other side still felt they needed to be mob-handed. Their fears were justified, as the Watney Street gang found when they waylaid Ron and me as we came out of a café in Commercial Road. We were surrounded by ten of these so-called tough guys. A mistake too many of these people make is thinking that a fight needs a bit of verbal pushing and shoving before the action. Not Ron and me. Before any of them knew what was happening, we'd reduced the odds down to three to one. Four of them reduced the odds even more when they ran away leaving their mates to take a good beating.

We spilt a lot of blood in those days but the sight of it never had the slightest effect on us. One of the reasons may have been that from when we were young children we had witnessed almost weekly the sight of badly injured people. We lived at the junction of Vallance Road and Dunbridge Street and it was notorious as an accident black spot. Cars, lorries and motorbikes ignoring the junction or not being aware of it until too late would speed across Vallance Road, resulting in some horrifying pile-ups. Every crash of metal on metal would bring us running with the morbid curiosity of the young. It might have been upsetting at first, but after a while we became quite immune to the sight of blood and smashed bodies. Family, neighbours and, in particular, Grandad Lee clamoured for something to be done and regularly petitioned the council. Grandad never had a day's schooling in his life but he could write a good letter. But nothing was done. Soaking up the outrage of the adults, we came to the conclusion that people were being hurt and killed because of the indifference of the authorities, so an unconscious rift was formed between us and the powers-that-be.

You may be forgiven for thinking that the violence I am describing was both gratuitous and unnecessarily bloody, and with the wisdom of hindsight I have to agree that perhaps it was. But those were the times we lived in. Sometimes violence is the only thing that some people understand. Being pulled up in front of the law and being given a few months inside does not always fit the crime, in my book. An example is of one time while walking back from the club I came across an old woman standing on her doorstep, wringing her hands, looking this way and that. I naturally stopped and enquired what was troubling her and it turned out that while she'd been shopping someone had entered her house and stolen a number of things, some of which were of great sentimental value. She knew who I was and I told her not to worry, I would see what I could do to help. Now there was not much that could be kept secret in the local area and so it was not difficult to find out who had been up to what. I put the word out and within hours had the name of the low-life youth who had robbed the old lady. I had him picked up and said that I wanted the stolen property brought with him. This was duly done. I had him taken to the old woman's house, where he not only handed back the goods but apologised and paid her some compensation. If he thought that that was all it took to reconcile his crime he had another thought coming. From there he was taken to the scrapyard by the club, given a severe beating, and then every finger on both hands was broken with an iron bar. It would be a long time before he was able to put his hands on other people's property and it would send out a message to those considering the same thing.

I have often heard it said that if Ronnie and I were still in the East End the crime figures would be drastically cut. That in itself is a compliment though I have to say, again from what I hear, that due to the high incidence of drug-taking and the rise of foreign gangs willing to kill for a wrong look, our own form of justice would be somewhat outdated.

However, sometimes our instinct to fight first, ask questions later backfired on us. One evening Ronnie had been in Pellicci's Café on the Roman Road with a few friends. They left and were standing outside the café talking and idly kicking at the slush on the pavement, when Ronnie was grabbed by the arm from behind. Instinctively he swung round and threw a punch at whoever had grabbed him. Unfortunately this turned out to be a copper, who, reeling back from the blow that had caught him on the shoulder, slipped on the icy pavement and sprawled full length on the ground. Ronnie helped him to his feet but he was already calling for back up. A police van arrived and Ronnie was kicked and punched into the back of it; the law doesn't like it when one of their own is assaulted. We heard that he'd been arrested later that evening, so me, Charlie and the old man – keeping his head well down – went to the station and demanded to see him. I couldn't believe my eyes when I caught sight of him. He had a lump the size of a golf ball on his forehead, his face was cut and bloody and his clothes were torn. He looked like he'd been in a road accident. He told us that a PC Baynton, the copper he'd knocked down, had been the instigator of the beating he'd received in the cell. There was nothing we could do at that stage to get Ron released, so we left. But as we walked up the road, PC Baynton, whom I knew, was walking towards us. I stepped in front of him and told him that I'd fucking well have him for what he'd done to my brother. He sneered at me and said, 'Just you try it and you'll get the same,' then turned away. I was in a rage at Ronnie's treatment so, without even considering the consequences, let fly a flurry of punches to his head, and leaving him holding his face, walked away. An hour later I was arrested at home and taken to join Ronnie. Mum was crying and Dad was doing his nut, but being on the run himself he couldn't strong it too much in case the law decided to dig out his file and lift him as well.

After a brief appearance at Old Street we found ourselves in a police van bound for remand in Wormwood Scrubs. We'd heard a whisper that if we kept quiet about the brutal beating Ron had received we could most probably get away with probation. So banking on the law keeping their side of the bargain, I wasn't too worried about the result. This allowed me to feel a lot of sympathy for the kids on the Borstal wing who had already been sentenced and were waiting for their allocation. I'd lie on my bed and listen to these kids calling to each other in loud whispers from the tiny cell windows.

'Whatcha get?'

'Three years. What about you?'

'Nine months.'

'Lucky bastard.'

'Got any snout?'

'Tommy's off to Hollesley Bay tomorrow.'

'That fat screw's a right fucker.'

The lights in the cells were switched off at nine o'clock but still the talking would go on far into the night. From the remand wing around me I'd hear muffled sobs as the dark hours cracked the veneer of daytime toughness and young villains cried for their mothers. Even though it's well over forty years ago, I can still picture the faces of those Borstal and remand boys I was banged up with and wonder what became of them all. As young as I was, with no conception of what the future held, I had a deep conviction that this would not be my last time behind the door.

When we eventually got to court, PC Baynton stood up and said in our defence that perhaps his over-reaction to the incident had caused the situation to get out of hand, and the assault was not quite as serious as it seemed. Absolute bollocks, but then he was under instruction to play it down in case the far more serious implication of police brutality came out in court. On top of his testimony came that of our friend, the well-respected vicar, Father Hetherington. We had known him for many years and had often helped him to run bazaars and fêtes at his church of St James in Bethnal Green.

He tried everything he could think of to try and get us to attend church services, but in the end gave up gracefully and just accepted the help we offered. Although he told the judge that he deplored our conduct, he also pointed out that basically we were honest lads who went out of our way to help others, particularly the elderly. Unlike the copper who said what he did without believing a word of it, Father Hetherington genuinely felt that what he was saying was the truth. And in a way it was, as far as he was concerned. The only trouble was, Ron and I lived two different lives – one the father saw and one he was not aware of.

At the end of the day we got a probation order against us, which meant we were free to leave the court. Although reporting every week to the probation officer would be a nuisance I think we were both pleased to get a result better than we could have hoped for.

With that bit of aggravation out of the way, brother Charlie felt that if we went to work with him he could keep his eye on us, and hopefully prevent us getting into any further trouble. So we became wardrobe dealers for a while but still managed to find a bit of trouble. We'd gone out to Chelmsford and spent the morning dropping flyers through letterboxes which said we'd call back in a couple of hours. We were just finished and were thinking of finding a café for a cup of tea, when a black van pulled up beside us and a tall fella of about thirty jumped out. He came up to me swearing and cursing, 'You ain't fucking buying round here, this is my patch so clear off.' I didn't argue, just swung a left hook to his chin and knocked him clean through a privet hedge. Funny thing was, all that could be seen was a large hole in the hedge with a pair of boots sticking out of it. After a spot of lunch we went back on the round and never saw anything of him.

Next time it was Charlie's turn, and he was supposed to be keeping us out of fights. We were working in the area of Eastcotes and had bought a fair amount of clothes, so each of us was carrying large black bags on our shoulders. As we passed a crew of workmen digging up the road, one of them shouted, 'Are you ladies taking your washing to the laundry?' He was about the same age as Charlie, very thick-set and stripped to the waist, and we could see he was covered in tattoos. Me and Ron were going to steam into him but Charlie told us that he would handle it. He went up to the fella and said, 'You've got a lot of mouth, let's see if you've got as much bottle.' The young bloke took up the challenge, but as he squared up Charlie knocked him to the ground. He scrambled up and was punched down again. Give him his due, he was game, but no match for our brother. In fact so quickly was he put down each time he never returned a single blow. We kept the rest of the workmen back in case they had ideas about helping their mate out, but it was soon over. Bruised and bleeding the fella put his hands up to show he'd had enough, so without a word Charlie put his jacket back on and we walked away.

For nine months or so we stuck it out, though more for Charlie's sake than our own. We were making a few quid but our hearts were just not in the clothes business, which was a bit of a blow to the old man who had started to think that all his sons would carry on the family tradition. As it turned out, if we'd waited a few weeks before jacking it in the decision would have been made for us anyway, as through the door came two buff envelopes ordering us to report for our national service.

6

Called Up, and Put Away

Our immediate response to getting the call up-for National Service was to take it on our toes, following another family tradition, but again with our best interests at heart our elder brother talked us out of it. He really believed that the tough training, manly lifestyle and an opportunity to follow an army boxing career would be the making of us. But as we began our service with an assault on a sergeant within hours of turning up at the Tower of London, the two years from March 1952 to March 1954 were to be a catalogue of disaster – for the army.

That first incident was nothing to do with arrogance, showing how tough we were or that we were bigger than the system. It was simply that we came to the conclusion that the Royal

Fusiliers wasn't for us and decided to leave. On the way out I gave a corporal, who had other plans for us, a smack on the chin that stretched him out on the floor. If we'd been serious about going on the trot we'd have been wise enough to have hidden up somewhere. As it was, we spent a good night up West and were ready for the law when they got us out of bed in Vallance Road at about five o'clock in the morning and whisked us off to Bethnal Green nick to await an army escort back to the Tower.

Crime – punishment – crime – punishment: it went on day after day as we made complete mugs out of the service. During one of our spells in detention a corporal opened up and said, 'C'mon Kray, visitor for you.'

I said, 'Is it my mother?'

He said, 'No, it's your Uncle George.' As I followed him I'm thinking, I haven't got an Uncle George. As I walked into the visitor's room, there's the old man sitting there with a big grin on his face giving me a wink. I couldn't believe it – he's still on the run himself and there he is inside the Tower of London, as cool as a cucumber.

Shortly afterwards Ron, myself and another young bloke, Dickie Morgan, walked out, this time with the intention of staying out. For a few days we stayed at Dickie's parents' house in Clinton Road at Mile End, but knowing the military police would turn up eventually, Ron and I headed back to Bethnal Green where we planned to keep out of sight. Making sure that the coast was clear we slipped in to see Mum for ten minutes, then took off for Hackney.

For a time we used Wallie's Café as a base. We'd sit about drinking tea and chatting to other young villains who might drop in. One of these was Ronnie Knight, who at the time of writing is banged up in Wandsworth Prison – but with a bit of luck, by the time you read this he'll be out and about on the London scene. Ronnie had an old taxi at the time and often we'd jump in the back and he'd drive us to the Royal Dance Hall in Tottenham for a good night out. When there was just the three of us he'd take us home to his mother's flat in Dalston and she'd cook us supper. His family were lovely people and always made us welcome.

We were by no means the only ones on the run from National Service. Some of the other fellas we knocked about with were Paddy Austen, Ronnie Diamond, who ran the Diamond gang, and Benny Robinson, whose brother was hanged for murdering a jeweller while robbing his shop in Bethnal Green Road.

We were all tucking into a meal of steak and chips in Wallie's Café, next door to the bus station in London Fields, when the door opened and in came a fella, immaculately dressed, five foot nine and heavily built. He had high cheekbones, a broken nose and brown eyes. As he took a seat, accompanied by two men and two women, conversation stopped as all eyes were on them. This was Tommy Smithson, a man liked and respected by all the young villains, not only around Hackney but all over London. He had a deserved reputation as a villain, gambler and fighting man. In fact he was what you might call a villain's villain, a legend, and part of the folklore of underworld London.

We had met him once before when we were with our old man, so when he caught sight of us he came over to our table and struck up a conversation. We explained our predicament of being almost skint and in need of a safe house and he immediately took out his wallet, peeled off a couple of notes, then took a key from another pocket and handed it to us. The key was to a spiel or gambling club he owned in Berwick Street, Soho. He said between the hours of 2 a.m. and 8 a.m. we could stay there for as many nights as we needed. A billiard table doesn't make the most comfortable bed, but with nothing better we'd no complaints.

This was typical of Tommy – he was a gentleman through and through. Born in Hackney, east London, Tommy was to all us young villains the type of man we would like to be, with his immaculate suits, jet-black American Buick and glamorous lifestyle. I often saw Tommy give money to down and outs and women of the street and they all thought the world of him. His generosity was an example to everyone.

But Tommy wasn't all good. At one time he'd slashed the throat of Fred 'Slip' Sullivan, one of Billy Hill's firm, so Billy and other members of the firm called a meet to talk things over. Tommy was always a loner, so he turned up at the pre-arranged spot on his own, but to balance things up a bit he'd armed himself with a revolver. He wasn't an idiot, but when Moishe Blueboy said the firm didn't want any more trouble, so why not shake hands, he went along with it and put the gun away. As soon as he did someone struck him across the back of the head with a hammer. Lying unconscious, he was so badly stabbed and cut by the Hill mob that one of his arms was almost severed. Attack over, he was put in the boot of Billy's car, then dumped near Hyde Park. As often happened in cases like that, a bit later a messenger from the firm turned up at the hospital and handed over an envelope containing £500. That was the underworld way. There had been a row, the debt was paid, now take a sweetener and keep your mouth shut. Tommy, being of the old school, handed back the money saying, 'Don't insult me, I know how the game's played.'

Three or four years later at the age of thirty-four he was found dead in the street with a bullet wound to the throat. Some time earlier he'd got into an argument over money he was owed by a gang boss by the name of Caruana. During the row in a Berner Street café, he cut the hands and arms of Caruana, then assuming he'd made his point, left. But he'd taken a liberty with the Maltese mafia and they had a contract put out on him.

Ron and I went to his funeral which took place at St Patrick's cemetery in Leytonstone. Prior to the funeral procession, we entered the little terraced house where Tommy lay in an open coffin and took a last look at him as we paid our last respects. He looked at peace and I noticed the hole in his neck had been plugged with cotton wool by the mortician.

Villains from all over London came to pay their respects and there were wreaths of all shapes and sizes placed on top of the cars, which stretched for half a mile in a long convoy. There was one wreath in the shape of a boxing ring, and another in the shape of a pair of dice showing snake's eyes to depict that Tommy's luck had finally run out.

This period on the run from the army was an education to both of us. In the preceding years we had built up a reputation, not only as skilful boxers but as fighters to steer clear of. We knocked about with some tasty young fellas and had more than a nodding acquaintance with many well-known villains on the manor. But really at this time we were more spectators than players in this tough and what seemed glamorous underworld life.

The fact that we had stuck two fingers up to the army seemed to give us a certain prestige and it was seen that Ron and myself didn't talk about what we would or wouldn't do, but were seen to carry out whatever we wanted to do. Soon we were being invited to join in with various criminal enterprises, which not only allowed us to dress in the style of successful villains, but put us in a position to rent a place in north London, which was far enough from Bethnal Green, where we knew the law was keeping an eye open for us, yet near enough to pop home under cover of darkness to see our family in the same way the old man had done for many years.

Returning to our flat in Finsbury Park one evening, we

spotted a police car outside. Their presence may have been nothing to do with us, but taking no chances we waited until they pulled away, cleared out our possessions and took off. This time we settled well away from our usual haunts in the alien country of south London. For a time we kept our heads down in a place just off Peckham Road in Southwark, but, as I said, the whole area was alien to us and a couple of months after our nineteenth birthday we made up our minds to spend Christmas at home and fuck the law. We got as far as the Red Café in Mile End, when one of life's coincidences reared its ugly head in the shape of PC Edward Fisher, who we'd had a run-in with a few years before. We stepped out of the café and there he was. If it had been a film we'd have said, 'Fair cop Guv'nor,' and gone in quietly, but it wasn't, so I gave him a shove that sent him sprawling across the slushy pavement, and we were away again.

I don't think the law took the apprehension of deserters too seriously, because if they'd put themselves out we could have been nicked nine months earlier. Their attitude seemed to be, why should we do the work of the military police? This was different though and they were not going to turn a blind eye to an assault on one of their own. Two weeks later we were both sitting in the Scrubs serving a month's sentence, and I could add another press cutting to my scrapbook. The headline 'Kray twins beat up PC' added to our status, even though it was a bit exaggerated. Inside, we were quite proud to be received by the other cons as celebrities and were able to make friendships with many of them that would last for years.

We knew what had to be faced as soon as the month was served, so it was no surprise when we found ourselves handcuffed and on our way to face a court-martial on the day of our release from Wormwood Scrubs. Again, we took it in our stride when we were sentenced to nine months and sent to Shepton Mallet. A bonus for us would come at the end of our time – dishonourable discharge.

You might think that it would have been in our own interests to knuckle down and accept the army way of life for two years instead of fighting against them for the same period of time, but that would have been impossible. For like our father and his father before him, there was no way we could bow to authority. At the same time, those two years were spent on the run doing just what we wanted to do. For a few months we ran riot in the fashion the army had come to expect from us until we reached a point where we felt we had nothing else to prove. We hadn't been beaten, but after a long discussion with each other about a future back in London, we decided the quicker we got there the better. So we kept our heads down and sat out the remaining months in a truce situation.

During the whole time we were in the army, there was only one man we had any respect for and that was a corporal by the name of Ted Haines. On one occasion Ron and I barricaded ourselves in a storeroom and refused to come out. The brass tried everything they could think of. They threatened us, sent in a load of sergeants and even a major, but we fucked them all off. Then Ted came to us, talked to us like men, which no one else had thought of, and said, 'Do me a favour, lads, and call it a day.' Put like that from a good man, how could we refuse? We were fed up with the game anyway. We got the guardhouse and he got a commendation. A week or so later he brought in his son, who was fourteen and a naval cadet. We had a laugh and a joke with him and he struck us as a good kid. When he left that day I never expected to see him again but forty years later he came to visit me here at Maidstone.

Within a short period of being discharged and returning to the East End, we began to put the career plan we'd discussed in our cell into action. We started to bring the gang back together. Among them was a likeable young bloke by the name of Ronnie Marwood, who could not have imagined that within a few years he would be put to death by hanging for the murder of PC Raymond Summers. Perhaps we could have imagined things would escalate as they did from the start.

Shortly after we were discharged from the army, I got into an argument with a fella in Lyons' Tea House at Aldgate. I can't remember his name but his father had a scrap metal business in Bow that paid a protection pension to Jack Spot who, in his own words, was 'King of the Underworld'. The argument escalated into the other fella squaring up to me. So I slipped a brass knuckle-duster onto my right hand and hit him in the face, breaking his jaw and most of his front teeth. A few days later, a whisper on the grapevine told me that the father, leaning on the fact of his weekly pension payment, had been to see Jack Spot in an effort to have us sorted out. We thought, OK, if Spotty wants to stick his nose in our business then he'll get a shock because we'll be ready for him.

We put the word out among our own team, contacted Johnny Nash and his firm for all of us to meet at Vallance Road on the following Sunday. Our collection of tools was still hidden under the bed at home, undisturbed while we'd been away. In no time at all everyone was kitted out with some form of weapon and forty-strong we headed for Ziggy's Café in Petticoat Lane where we knew Jack and his mob would be. As there was so many of us, I suggested we split up and spread out just in case we caught the eye of the law. By way of an anti-climax Jack Spot never showed – perhaps his grapevine warned him to keep his head down or he and his followers would have been cut to pieces.

On reflection, I was pleased that the intended row never happened because both Ron and I became friends with all those men we might have hurt. Without effort I can recall their names today. George and Jimmy Woods, Teddy Machin, Little Jackie Reynolds, and Ted and Bill Robbins, all from Upton Park. From Aldgate was Moishe Blueboy and from Whitechapel, the little Jew, Arnie Rosen. Another of

Spotty's men, Sonny the Yank, would some time later join the ranks of that exclusive club of eleven men whose jaws I would break.

Our first career move, though not planned as such, was to place us on the threshold of unimaginable heights that would eventually lead us to wealth, power, notoriety and, subsequently, a lifetime's imprisonment. But as we handed over a fiver for the first week's rent on the run-down Regal Billiard Hall, in Eric Street, all that was in our minds was now we had a base more business-like than our bedroom in Vallance Road, and at the same time we could be earning a few quid. To be honest, when we walked in on that first day it looked a daunting prospect. The place was a hole. It was dirty, dingy and the dozen billiard tables were grey under accumulated cigarette ash. I've never been afraid of hard graft, as long as it's in my own interests, so with plenty of elbow grease, soapy water and a few gallons of paint, the place was transformed within a couple of weeks. A fitted bar and a delivery of drinks added the final touch, and we were in business.

There was a bonus to our Eric Street premises. To one side was a small scrapyard, which we farmed out for rent, and to the front was a large forecourt where we'd soon be selling cars. In fact, one of the first cars we bought for resale was a Ford Austin that was built in 1900 and looked like a toy. I sold it to a Pakistani man for a small sum, yet today that same car would be worth thousands. Being in the trade, even though it was only in a small way, allowed me to buy on the cheap, and from that time I owned so many cars for my personal use that I truly forget how many or what they were. But some of my favourites still come easily to mind. One of the best was a bottle-green Mercedes Benz 220/SE two-door saloon. It was beautiful inside and out, which was to be expected as I paid £5,000 for it in 1963. I must have looked like royalty, which never failed to bring a smile to my face as, whenever I drove through London, policemen on point duty would salute as they waved me through an intersection. Another car of royal appearance was an Austin Shireline, though for speed nothing could touch my American Ford Galaxy.

I loved speeding but it often ended in minor crashes. A Sprite sports car was so low to the ground that I ripped the bottom out of it on the kerb outside one of our clubs. More serious was when I was speeding through Mile End in my usual reckless style. A lorry braked sharply and the Vanguard I was driving ploughed into the back of it. The motor was wrecked and I had to be cut free and carted off to the hospital in Bancroft Road in Stepney. I still bear the scar from six stitches in my elbow. From the hospital I went straight to the Double R Club. With my bandages, cuts, bruises and a very swollen face due to a penicillin allergy, a lot of people thought I'd been in a fight. They should have known better, for without false modesty I can in all honesty say that in all the fights Ron or I had, and they number hundreds, neither of us was ever cut or received broken bones.

Apart from the car lot at the front of the Regal, I fenced off a corner for privacy and invited two very special friends of ours, Dot and Tommy Walsh, to pull in their caravan and live without aggravation from the authorities. Ron and I first met Tommy Walsh – sometimes known as Tommy Brown, but most often as Tommy 'The Bear' – when we went to a gym in Tottenham where he did a bit of sparring. I know 'gentle giant' is a bit of a cliché, but I can't think of a better way to describe him. Well over six foot tall, twenty stone in weight, his white hair, genial humour and battered good looks brought to mind that famous screen heavy Victor McLaglen. At that time he was taking on all-comers in the booths and it wasn't long before we were accompanying him to fights and, when it suited us, jumping in the ring to earn ourselves a few quid, though not against our friend Tommy. Though he could have smashed anyone who took a liberty or got out of order, he'd avoid that drastic action, preferring to hold the offender upside down by his ankles, place a foot gently on their chin saying, 'C'mon – be nice.'

Uncle Joe was a good mate of Tommy's back in the twenties and always spoke fondly of him. Apparently they were both training one night in the gym when two coppers came in looking for Mr Brown. Tommy looked at them a bit cross-eyed but said, 'That's me, what's the problem?' They said, 'This isn't business. We're training up for a Police Federation match and wondered if we could have the gloves on with you.' Tommy agreed. The first one got in the ring and straight off got such a blow in the face that it knocked some of his teeth out. A lot of people thought it was done maliciously because the guy was a copper but the truth is Tommy didn't know his own strength sometimes.

When I first met Tommy and his wife they were living in their eighteen-foot trailer on a bomb-site in Salmon Lane. Whenever I got the opportunity, I'd slip up there and hope to be invited to stay overnight. It may have been the gypsy part of me but I loved the cosiness of their compact little caravan. At the time, I thought my hints to stay over were quite subtle, but long after Dot said to me, 'We knew what you were after. You'd sit there fidgeting, wriggling your feet about and yawning, just waiting for me to say stop over if you want.' My excuse was that the trains passing Vallance Road kept me awake but as she pointed out, her caravan was even closer to the railway line. Unfortunately the council eventually forced them from the site, which was when I suggested they move to Eric Road.

I'm proud to say that Dot thought the world of Ron and me and would do anything for us. When Ron was away, Dot was asked to take care of a few of his personal effects. Among them were two large bags of shirts, and being the woman she was she took it upon herself to wash and iron every single one so Ron had something nice waiting for him on the outside. They were mostly dress shirts with frilled front and cuffs – a nightmare to work on. But because they were Ron's she persevered and did half a dozen at a time whenever she had a spare moment. For days that woman must have toiled over those shirts, but she never complained. One day, a close friend of Ron's, Teddy Smith, called in to see that Dot was all right. She gave him a cup of tea and they were having a chat, when all of a sudden Teddy burst into tears. Horrified, Dot asked him what was the matter. He pointed to the shirts and said, 'No one has ever been so kind to me in my whole life.' Dot nearly fell over; they were not Ron's shirts.

As close to us as Tommy was, he was never on the firm as a heavy and minder. He was just a man who enjoyed our company and looked upon us as his sons. In fact, when the law started breathing down our necks, Tommy kept away from us – even though it hurt him to do so – in case his own record caused us trouble. After we were sent down he was even more hurt when his letters to us were returned and he was threatened with imprisonment if he continued to contact us.

In later years Tommy sadly suffered a mental breakdown and spent some years in an institution until his wife Dot, even though they had been separated for many years, decided to bring him home to Tottenham. Because of his illness he spent his days silent and uncommunicative. But he'd always loved our mother and when a picture of her and news of her death came on the television, he came out of his shell and shouted, 'SHE WAS A GOOD WOMAN.'

When he passed away himself, a special coffin had to be made because of his size. At the graveside where cameras and reporters were clamouring for a view, the Catholic priest commented to Dot that he must have been very famous. She replied, 'No . . . just an ordinary man who lived his life the way he wanted to.' I know I can speak for Ron when I say that today Dot Walsh is our most special friend.

The billiard hall was proving to be a winner and we were earning good money, but being the person I was I liked to have as many irons in the fire as possible and nothing gave me greater pleasure than earning a few quid on the side, particularly if the venture was a scam. One that never failed involved the use of supposedly snide (counterfeit) banknotes. I'd look out for a mug with more greed than sense and steer the conversation round to dodgy money. I wouldn't push him too hard, just hint that I could lay my hands on a fair amount for the right person. His casual attitude as he asked where he could see some of this money made me laugh because I could see he was eager to make a few bob. Not surprisingly, I would just happen to have a few samples in my wallet, and with an air of great furtiveness I'd pull out a wad of crisp five-pound notes that I'd drawn from the bank that day. His eyes would pop, 'I've never seen snide notes as good as these, ever.' Of course he hadn't realised they were genuine and uncirculated. At thirty shillings each, we'd agree that he wanted to spend a monkey (£500) and I'd set up a meet for the handover. For this I would need an accomplice, for as I handed over the tightly sealed packet of cut-up newspaper in return for his cash, someone would have to say, 'Look up, Old Bill's coming.' In the panic the punter would take off without discovering his mistake. By the time he did it would be too late – much too late.

Another good earner was with the help of a crooked doctor we knew. This doctor had a practice in the Millwall Dock area. A friend of ours, Billy Jones, introduced us to the Doc after telling us that for a fee, he could get young lads rejected from doing their compulsory National Service, which was in force at the time. Needless to say, we latched onto that racket a bit lively. Once word got around, we had loads of seventeen-year-olds turning up at the Regal looking to be declared medically unfit. It might have saved us and the army a lot of aggravation if we'd met him a few years earlier.

The Doc was a man who could be trusted, so eventually we took him on the firm to help out on matters where straight doctors might have tipped off the law. When he was needed, he could invariably be found playing cards and gambling in the Green Dragon Social Club throughout the early hours. If he wasn't at the tables he'd be in an armchair fast asleep, still wearing an overcoat. I'd shake him by the shoulder and say, 'I've just shot a bloke in a club at Highbury and he's got two bullets in his leg. Can you come and sort it?' And up he'd get up, still half asleep, and follow me without a murmur. That particular geezer had got well out of order over a civil request for him to quieten down in the club. A few heated words were exchanged and he pulled a knife on me. I had a small-calibre pistol in my jacket pocket so pulled it out and let him have two shots in the leg. I aimed for his legs because I had no intention of killing him but it did the job of slowing him down. Then I had the aggravation of calling up the Doc to render him first aid. A footnote to that was a few weeks later he came back to the club and apologised for his behaviour.

Another time I hit a fella on the chin during an argument in the billiard hall, and down he went, spark out. I turned away, but as I did so a friend, Tommy Fluck, who I believe was a relative of the lovely Diana Dors, took it on himself to make sure the fella stayed unconscious and whacked him over the head with a billiard cue as he lay on the floor. The intention wasn't to kill him, so it was another call to the Doc who came out right away, brought the bloke round and put six stitches in his head while he was still groggy.

Much later when we were arrested for murder, the police threatened and harassed the Doc in an effort to make him disclose what he knew about us. But true member of the firm that he was, he couldn't be intimidated and remained silent. This great character is dead now, but if he's listening up there, Doc, you were a real man who always had my respect.

Following the success of the Regal and discovering we had a natural flair for this line of business, we soon expanded into similar areas. Eventually we owned or had part shares in clubs in many different parts of London, ranging in style and clientele, from Soho to Knightsbridge. Esmeralda's Barn, our gambling club, or spiel as it was known, was a showpiece and managed by our uncle, Alf Kray, at 50 Wilton Place, Knightsbridge. It was situated in the right area to attract exclusive customers such as the aristocracy, politicians, bankers and similar types from the moneyed set. Dress suits and evening wear were common, while the players at roulette, chemin-de-fer and cards were quiet and respectable. In fact I can only remember one instance of trouble and that was an ugly scene when Uncle Alf had to knock out a drunken nuisance.

Because we were in the business of encouraging big spenders to relax and enjoy themselves, drinks and food were given free. While making sure everything ran smoothly we would mingle with out guests dressed in similarly expensive clothes. Ron would wear a black dress suit, white shirt and bow tie. Charlie and myself usually wore light-blue mohair dress suits, white shirts and blue bow ties. We all looked what we were – successful club owners.

In extreme comparison were the punters that frequented our club in Willington Way, Bow. Sometimes I'd look at them and think that the language, appearance and facial expressions were quite Dickensian. Most of these customers were of rough manners, dockers, ex-fighters and criminals, and would have come on to the club after closing time at the Double R or billiard hall. These East End gamblers rarely welshed on a gambling debt – for two reasons. One was that within this circle they behaved with honesty while giving us respect. The second reason was that they were wise enough to realise that they would face dire consequences if they tried it on.

Our philosophy was simple. When the punter won, he or she would be paid out immediately without any fuss. Likewise, when lady luck was against them we expected them to return the compliment. Strangely enough, we had to send the debt collectors after more of the rich clientele of Esmeralda's Barn than in any of the less affluent spiels. Rarely was violence necessary. Usually all it took was a quiet word from the right person to replace a bounced cheque with cash.

Apart from making good money out of a business we enjoyed, it gave us an opportunity to mix and become friends with famous personalities from all over the world who sought out our venues, having heard they were the in-place to be. Not only did we meet them as clients but some would visit us at home, while others would go out with us to various clubs, functions and shows as friends. Sophie Tucker, the famous 'Red Hot Mamma', was one that often came to Vallance Road. She thought a lot of Ron and if she ever needed advice she'd park her Rolls-Royce outside our little terraced house and come in for a cup of tea and a chat with him.

Like most women my mum had been a fan of the French singer and actor Charles Boyer since the 1930s. So when we heard he was coming to London, my brother Ron sorted out an introduction. This grey-haired heart-throb bowed to her with his Gallic charm and kissed her hand. I can still picture my mother's face: she was so thrilled.

Rocky Marciano, Joe Louis, Barbara Windsor, Lionel Bart and Joan Littlewood – the names go on and on. One of the nicest and most down-to-earth people was the late Judy Garland. She must have been the number-one actress/singer in the whole world, yet the night she came to our club she made a bee-line for our cousin Rita to admire the coat she was wearing at close quarters. Strangers until that moment, the pair of them sat most of the evening talking 'girl talk'. Her parting words to Rita were, 'I would love my daughter Liza to meet you, you are such a nice person.'

Rita was Aunt May's daughter, some years younger than us and someone we always looked on as the sister we might have had. As a teenager she was beautiful and, like her mother, blonde. We were always proud to escort her to parties, dances or clubs. However, apparently I had not always felt like this. Though I was too young to remember the incident, I'm told that when I was three I nearly did away with Rita. My mother and aunts Rose and May were in the kitchen when I came in from the backyard smacking my fat little hands together as though I'd just put the world to rights. All they could get out of me were the words, 'I dunnit, I dunnit.' Puzzled as to what I had 'dun' they went out the back to find Rita trapped under her pram, though fortunately unhurt. I'd obviously been proud of the fact that singlehandedly I'd managed to turn over such a large object. She didn't bear a grudge, because when she got a bit older she was always pestering her mother to take her to see the 'two ones', her way of summing up twins.

Cousin Rita had a talent for dressmaking and after leaving school she applied for and got a job as a royal seamstress. Who knows what heights she could have reached within the royal circle, but it wasn't to be. Her mother wouldn't let her take up the post, saying she wasn't having her travelling into the heart of London every day with all these strange men about, so Rita, with a respect that seems to be lacking in youngsters of today, gave up her dream and had to settle for a job in a local factory.

Her father was one of the nicest men you could ever meet. He'd done his share in the war, yet he was so decent I found it hard to imagine that he was capable of pulling the trigger of a gun. Off the battlefield Uncle Albert was no fighter but he was game. Rita was getting ready for bed one night when she noticed someone bending down behind her father's car. She called downstairs, 'Dad, there's a big man doing something to your car.' Albert pulled on some trousers over his pyjamas and went out. The fella had parked his own car further down the road, and as soon as he saw Albert he made a run for it. Albert chased him and there was a bit of a scuffle and that's when I came into the picture. I was just coming home from somewhere when I saw the two of them struggling. It was dark but I recognised my uncle so I grabbed the other bloke by the throat and asked them what was going on. Albert said, 'This bloke was trying to nick my hub caps.' By this time, as big as he was, the fella had gone to pieces and was saying how sorry he was. I didn't know him but I think he must have recognised me. He even pulled some money out and offered it. All I said was, 'I think you've been a bit out of order. Don't let me see you round here again.' He looked relieved to have got off so lightly. Then I hit him as hard as I could on the side of his jaw. Uncle Albert and I walked away and I can't be sure if his jaw was broken so I have never added it to the eleven I *am* sure of. If it wasn't, it must have been made of steel.

Uncle Albert was a quiet man, unlike his wife, Aunt May, who was a complete extrovert. She took after her father and if anyone should have been on the stage it was her. She was the life and soul of parties or in the pub and needed no excuse to sing, do high kicks or show off for everyone's amusement with gesticulations or comical facial expressions and mannerisms. She thought a lot of Ron and me and when we were with her would say to anyone in the vicinity, friend or passerby, 'Don't you think these twins are fine and handsome boys?'

Uncle Albert died in 1986 and two years later our lovely happy-go-lucky Aunt May followed him. Her death certificate said heart attack, but Dr Hardy, who had been looking after her, said it was a broken heart.

Thinking about Rita and her family reminds me that like Ron and me, she loved pets of all kinds. She was always picking up something or other, so much so that her mother would have to warn her every morning, 'Don't you bring any cats, dogs or birds home tonight.' A Jack Russell dog followed her home one time, or so she said.

'Mum, can I keep it?'

'No it belongs to someone,' Aunt May replied.

Rita pleaded so May said, 'All right then, if I open the door and it goes out, that's it. But if it stays you can keep it.' She opened the door and the dog took a couple of steps towards it then had second thoughts. Rita quickly slammed the door shut before it changed its mind, and May gave in and let her keep it. Rita didn't always have such luck with her pets. She once bought a tortoise and when she showed it to Nan Lee, Nan said, 'Make a nice ashtray that would.' Never found out if Nan got her way.

Another time I had bought an Alsatian to guard the Carpenter's Arms, a pub we owned. We had a manager running the place and after a while I noticed the dog was looking a bit thin. I felt it wasn't being fed as it should have been, so I gave it to Aunt May and gave her money every week for its keep. She named it Rex. The dog was trained to bring down Rita's cup and saucer from her bedroom, one at a time. As all the houses in Vallance Road had outside toilets, May, being a bit old-fashioned, would put a chamber pot under her bed. She never used it but how could she tell that to the decorators who were in the house when Rex came down the stairs, handle of the pot firmly in his mouth, and placed it at her feet. The dog thought it was a big cup.

Rex eventually proved himself as the guard dog he was bought to be. Two blokes were acting a bit suspiciously at the back of our house. Albert let the dog out and it pinned one of them to the wall. He's shouting, 'Get it off me,' and Albert's shouting, 'You've got no right here, what are you up to?' They were plain-clothes coppers.

Brave as that dog was it would never go into May's front room, no matter how much they tried to coax him. Nobody was more level-headed than Rita but she had a good idea why – as far as she was concerned the place was haunted. I have no reason to doubt her, for with gypsy in her blood she may well have inherited sensitivity for such things. On one occasion she saw a little old lady wearing an old-fashioned dress with a high collar. Her hair was in a rolled-up style and she wore a very distinctive brooch. When she told her mother she said it sounded like old Mrs Doyle, a previous occupant who'd been dead for years.

Years later Rita moved into a flat and had to give Rex away. Every time she carved some meat she'd cry, thinking of how she'd always given him the first piece.

Ron and I had pets from when we were small kids right up until we were put away. We had budgerigars, canaries, chickens, mice, rabbits, a couple of boa constrictors we named after two policemen, Gerrard and Read, and I even had a small monkey that I'd bought in a pet shop in Camden Town. One of the funniest pets we had was a mynah bird we called Jackie. It was jet-black with a yellow beak and when it suited itself it would shout, 'Let's go out and get some money.' It would also mimic a cough our old man had. You'd hear, 'Hrm, hrm, hrm,' and half the time we wouldn't know who was doing it – the old man or the bird. Most of the time if you said, 'What's your name?' it would say, 'Bollocks.' Or if it was asked, 'Who's a lovely boy?' back would come the reply, 'Bollocks.' Jackie loved saying this word and nearly caused some trouble when we were having a meeting at Vallance Road.

Charlie, Ron and I often acted as peacemakers if trouble flared up between rival families. Talking through us as inter-mediaries, problems could be resolved without either side losing face. On this particular occasion the birdcage was cov-ered up, so Jackie's piercing whistle wouldn't disturb us, and the meeting with the two firms was going well towards a sat-isfactory conclusion. Then Albert Smith made some point and from under the blanket Jackie said, 'Bollocks.' I thought Albert was going to blow a fuse. He shoved his chair back and glared at his former enemies, thinking someone was taking the piss. But before he could blow up, I whipped the cover off the cage and let him see the bird. He looked a bit dubious until, on cue, Jackie looked at him and as usual said, 'Bollocks.' The meeting ended in good humour.

My favourite pet, and looking back the one I miss most of all, was Mitzy, a Pekinese. That dog went everywhere with me and it was a very sad day when she was run over and killed on a caravan site near Southend.

7

Frances

Of all the things that bought me happiness, it was my late wife Frances who was my greatest joy. This is a poem I wrote about my feelings for her.

We had our joy and sorrow
We did not think about tomorrow
Each day was new and fun
Our love had a good run
We were so in love
Such love could only be sent from above
The magic was in her large brown eyes
And beautiful smiles
She was meant for me

She was everything I wished to see
She was just sixteen
I was twenty-six years
And I did not foresee the tears
Because we were so happy
But the tears came and life
Was no longer a game
We had both the joy and sorrow
Yesterday was not like tomorrow
Our teenage love is no more
We had not counted on what was in store
The girl with the beautiful eyes
And smiles was no more
This is what life had in store
I will not forget those eyes and smile
They remain part of my memory forever
How can I forget such a smile
I'm sad but can say I've known
True love and will remember her beautiful eyes
She is somewhere in the skies
So our love remains above
Maybe our love will begin again tomorrow.

I first met Frankie Shea, brother to Frances, when I decided to look for a different car than the Vanguard I was driving at the time. He had a car lot in north London and although he had nothing that suited me, we struck up a friendship that led to him becoming my driver. He was about eighteen years of age, a good-looking kid with brown eyes, dark hair and an olive complexion. As a driver he was the best I had come across, while his personality made him exceptional company. Some time after we met I got caught up in an amateurish, so-called protection racket that was nothing to do with me whatsoever. The details are unimportant other than, a con man and fraudster, who'd never been known to use violence, had struck a shopkeeper, demanded money and threatened him. Without knowing anything about what had gone on I happened to be with him the day he called back to collect his money. The police were waiting and we were both arrested. What a fiasco! For once I was innocent but was looking at a couple of years inside. I spent a few months on remand in Wandsworth until I was released on bail pending my appeal against conviction.

Needing a driver to ferry me around while I sorted out various bits of business, I made my way to 57 Ormsby Street in Shoreditch where Frankie lived. I knocked on the door and when it opened there stood the most beautiful girl I had ever seen. I hadn't known of her existence because to Frankie she was just his kid sister and not worth talking about. As I gazed into her large brown eyes, her innocent face framed by chestnut hair, I fell deeply in love for the first time. She was sixteen and I was twenty-six, and from that day I courted her in a way that some might say was old-fashioned – with courtesy, respect, flowers and chocolates.

When I went back to court to have my appeal heard, it was rejected and I was sent back to Wandsworth for six months. Believe me when I say that those six months were harder to serve than the twenty-six years that were to come. I was tortured daily by thoughts of Frances – perhaps she would meet someone else or perhaps she wouldn't wait for me. On top of that I clashed with Frankie Shea over the fact that he wanted to take his sister to nightclubs in my absence.

One night he took her to Freddie Foreman's club in south London. When they turned up at the door Fred told him he was not welcome to bring Frances in as it was against his principles for her to be nightclubbing while I was in prison. I heard recently on the grapevine that Frankie is still in the car game and has a grey head of hair. On reflection I can only remember the good times we had together and should he read this I would like to wish him all success and happiness in the future.

The day I was released from Wandsworth was the beginning of the happiest years of my life. I took Frances to the Astor Club, close to Berkeley Square, and I'll never forget how she looked that night as the soft candlelight reflected on her face. I bought a teddy bear wrapped in cellophane and presented it to Frances as a small token of my love. In time I would buy her expensive clothes, jewellery and cars, but none was treasured more than that first gift. We left the club at 3 a.m., parked outside her house in Ormsby Street and kissed and cuddled until the windows steamed up, which amused her very much. We spoke of love and I told her how I was fighting to reach a life of glamour and bright lights. I was proud of my east London roots, but it was a jungle that I wanted to get out of and I wanted her to share my journey towards a better life.

My mother and father treated her like a daughter, and if I had to be out on business she was quite happy to sit talking and drinking tea with them. Frances and Cousin Rita also hit it off and they would spend hours shopping in the West End.

We had wonderful holidays in all parts of the world but Frances was the kind of person who could be happy whether we were in Tangiers, the caravan at Southend or the kitchen in Vallance Road. I can remember when our friend Ronald Stafford drove us to the South of France for a holiday. Whether we were tired or irritable from the hot sun I can't remember, but like lovers invariably do at some time, we had an argument while sitting outside a bistro. This became heated, resulting in Frances saying, 'You're nothing outside of the East End. You're not known here in France or anywhere else in the world.' I was very hurt by her assumption that I was arrogant enough to believe I was some sort of international celebrity. Our tiff soon passed but I slight very easily, and her words had the effect of spurring me on towards an ambition to be known in a circle much larger than my own.

Eventually Frances and I were married in the April of 1965. This was in St James the Great church, Bethnal Green, known as the Red Church because of its red-brick façade. An interesting fact about this church was that to encourage people to get married it did so without charge. Once the ceremony was over the couple were given a loaf of bread and sixpence. When it was our turn we didn't have to pay and the bread and coin had long been abandoned.

Just over two years later I buried Frances at Chingford Cemetery. My beautiful, innocent wife was dead and part of me died with her. Our few years spent together were in the main happy but, like many young lovers, we had our differences. She never really took to the club scene, which was my livelihood, but would rather spend time at home or with my family. I think she resented the time I had to spend on my many business dealings. At the same time Ronnie never took to her in the way I would have liked him to have done. The reasons never fully came out into the open, though I suspect he felt she came between our close bond. Certain personal details came out at her inquest and all I can say in my defence is that I put her on far too high a pedestal. Instead of accepting she was an ordinary, if remarkably beautiful, girl I imbued her with an almost ethereal quality which possibly put a strain on this sensitive person. In the months following her death there were so many times when I wanted to join her, cowardly as that may seem, but life goes on no matter how painfully. My intention was to write of our days together in depth but lifting the veil on that part of my life has proved too painful to remember.

If only we could have both youth and wisdom at the same

time. If I could turn the clock back there are many things I would do differently. I fell out with Frankie and quarrelled many times with Frances's parents, which in hindsight was very sad. Life is too short to spend it in recriminations, yet it is easy to have a greater understanding looking back. Frances was a lover of poetry, so I am sure she would appreciate the words of compassion, love and friendship as written by the prophet Khalil Gibran. His work and the sentiments he conveys are among my favourite writings. A short verse he wrote reminds me so much of my parting from her.

When you part from your friend, you grieve not:
For that which you love in him may be clearer in his absence, as the mountain to the climber is clearer from the plain.

8

Around the Manor, and Beyond

With business interests spread so far and wide around town, we would regularly visit a number of venues in the course of an evening. And of course, we'd inevitably meet up with associates from the underworld along the way.

Mike Connors could be seen any day of the week outside Holborn tube station, where he had a flower stall. He was an unmistakable figure with a face like an underground map due to the deep razor scars all over it. Mike had always been a villain and at one time had been attacked and cut badly outside White City Dog Track. He could always be seen at the big fights in the company of my friends Alex Stean and the late Jack 'Kid' Berg.

Further east on the Central line, a common sight in

Bethnal Green was two local villains, Willy and Johnny Collins, chatting away while leaning on the railings outside the tube station. At one time Willy was at a gambling club in the Aldgate area when he had an argument with Harry Lazar, the ex-pro lightweight fighter. He knew that he would have no chance in a fist fight with Lazar so he hit him over the head with a billiard cue. For many years Johnny visited Ron at Broadmoor and Ron was very upset when he died a few years ago.

If I travelled north from Holborn to the Senate Rooms Club at Highbury I would be met at the entrance to the club by one of my favourite villains and oldest friends, Steve Murphy. He had the looks of a younger version of the former President of the United States, Ronald Reagan, and he dressed just as good as Reagan. Steve, like Patsy Arragon, was a good club host and there was hardly any trouble on his premises. He was one of the top money-getters of his day and had been brought up through the ranks of villainy with such people as Big Alf Murvin, Tommy Smithson and Tony Mulla, so he had been in good company.

If I looked around the Senate Rooms I might have seen Tommy Cowley sitting at the bar with a drink in his hand and chain-smoking while he chatted away with one of the club hostesses. Tommy was another good friend of ours and was given a nine-month sentence for harbouring Frank Mitchell after we'd got him out of Dartmoor Prison. Tommy was about five foot six in height and slightly built. He had ginger hair and was a neat dresser. He was a compulsive gambler and spent most of his time in gambling spiels. Later on he would spend four years behind these same walls here at Maidstone.

Further east again, if I took a drive over to Queen's public house on the corner of Upton Park at any time in the 1960s, I would expect to see gathered at the bar a group of men who called themselves the Upton Park Mob. They would all be there, Jimmy and Georgie Woods, Porky and Dickie Bennett, Little Jackie Reynolds, Ted Machin, Ted and Billy Robbins and if it was a good night the villains' villain, Billy Hill. Joining them after a seven-year stretch behind the wall would be Porky Bennett, just released from Dartmoor. He had been convicted of razor-slashing someone and demanding money with menaces from Chinese restaurant owners in the area of Pennyfields in Chinatown. Porky would be immaculate in a single-breasted suit, waistcoat, white shirt and dark tie and topped off with a smart trilby hat that would have graced a gangster movie. Terry Robbins would be wearing a smart raincoat and a checked cloth cap. Jimmy and Georgie would look their usual immaculate selves and dangling from Jimmy's waistcoat would be a gold chain with a neat pocket watch attached. Little Jackie Reynolds would be sitting at one of the tables in the corner of the bar and one couldn't help noticing that he had a jagged scar on the left side of his face. His alert little brown eyes would be taking in all that he saw.

Travelling around our manor wasn't always just meeting up with associates. Occasionally we had to step in and sort out the trouble. It was during this period that we had a gambling club at Wellington Way, back towards our manor in Bow Road. Georgie Woods and Jackie Reynolds along with Limehouse Willie ran the club for Charlie, Ron and me. One day at the club Jackie had an argument with Buster Osbourne, who had been a successful professional welterweight. I was in the club that day and I noticed them having words, then I saw Jackie walk away and sit down at a table with Sammy Josephs. Sammy had recently finished a ten-year sentence in Dartmoor for his part, along with Jimmy and Georgie Woods, in the London Airport gold bullion robbery. Keeping my eye on Jackie, I saw him get up from the table and go to the fireplace in the centre of the room, pick up a poker and push it deep into the glowing coals. I went over to him and asked him what the problem was and he said, 'I'll show the bastard if he wants trouble. I'll show him.' Buster was also a friend of mine and I didn't want trouble in my club, so as diplomatically as I could and without Jackie losing face, I managed to persuade him not to carry out his threat. If trouble had flared there was no doubt that he was more than capable of doing what he intended.

Crossing the Mile End Road and heading north, I might stop at the the Spread Eagle pub on the corner of Shoreditch, the drinker used by Alfie Allpress and Nobby Clark. Alf was over six foot tall and broad, while in contrast Nobby was quite short. Nobby had served a couple of sentences for theft and violence and he was a friend of Frankie Fraser and Johnny Collins. Alf, whom I shared some time with in Parkhurst, carried a lot of weight in criminal circles and was respected by all.

Of course, Soho was a glamorous destination at the time, and we'd often end up there. Sometimes I would go to a club run by Peter Gillam and his brother and have a drink with my friend, Alfie Gerard. Alfie came from Canning Town and was well known all over London for being a good gunman. One time he'd pulled a shooter on Buller Ward when they had a flare-up while drinking in a club down the meat market. This was not a liberty on his part as Buller himself was a very capable villain and hard man. In fact, I had a run-in with him myself at the Regency Club. We had a disagreement that ended with me giving him a right hand punch on the chin. As he staggered back, I pulled a German flick-knife out of my pocket and cut him across the side of the face, opening his face up from the corner of his eye to his mouth. Looking after my interests, Roy Nash, who was in the club at the time, bolted the door to stop anyone leaving and perhaps calling the police. There was blood all over Buller's royal blue suit and on the foyer carpet, but with the business done I had him taken to the London Hospital where he needed a hundred stitches to pull his face together. Looking back I'm not proud of such violence, but they were the times we lived in and, given the chance, he would have done to me what he'd done to many others.

Leaving Alf and the Gillam brothers I would probably head for the Pigalle Club, just off Regent Street to see Scotch Jack Buggy. He'd be sitting at a table close to the stage where Shirley Bassey would be captivating the audience with her singing. Jack was a very flash villain and at one time he'd been given a ten-year sentence when he was convicted of shooting Big Charlie Reader in the stomach outside the Pigalle Club. Charlie was lucky to live, but some years later Buggy went missing and was never seen again. As I've said, memories are very long in the underworld.

The Pen Club was a favourite East End haunt for many villains. It was situated in an upstairs building in the vicinity of Spitalfields Market. During the early hours the patrons would start to drift in with the assurance that genial company and a relaxed atmosphere awaited them. It wasn't renowned for being a trouble spot, in fact quite the opposite, which accounted for its popularity at this hour of the day. During one particular drinking session, an altercation started between the club owners, Jimmy Cooney and Billy Ambrose, and some customers, who were not members. They were led by Jimmy Nash, who had seven brothers. Jimmy was a well-known figure in the London underworld and had a certain reputation. He was of strong build with a thick bull neck and sported a short-cropped crew-cut hairstyle. Others in his party that night were Joe Pyle and John Reed. Reed was the son of a Croydon policeman and, like Pyle, had once been a professional fighter. Billy Ambrose was well known as an ex-middleweight professional fighter and at the time he was on parole after serving a prison sentence at Dartmoor. He'd been sentenced to a term of eleven years for stealing a large quantity of gold pens from a warehouse, which explains how the Pen Club got its name.

The argument in the Pen Club was beginning to escalate. As Cooney and Ambrose advanced towards Jimmy Nash to try to calm the situation down and prevent any further incident, it was alleged that Nash removed a German Mauser pistol from his coat pocket and fired point-blank at the approaching men. Jimmy Cooney was hit in the chest and Billy Ambrose caught it in the stomach. Cooney staggered down the stairs to the dimly lit street, blood gushing from the wound in his chest. Then his balance gave way and he keeled over to fall in the gutter. His girlfriend rushed to him and cradled his head, but the shot proved to be fatal and Jimmy Cooney died where he lay. Billy Ambrose had the presence of mind to jump in his car and drive to the London Hospital where emergency surgery saved his life. The fact that Ambrose had kept his body in peak condition and was extremely fit and healthy probably contributed to his recovery.

After the fatal shooting, Jimmy Nash, Joe Pyle and John Reed left the Pen Club and headed straight for my mother's house in Vallance Road to seek assistance from Ron and me. They told us they were in a bit of trouble, which we thought was the understatement of the year! Jimmy Cooney had once managed a drinking club for Aggie Hill, the wife of Billy Hill, before they divorced, so we were familiar with Cooney and his girlfriend. Also Ron and I had always had a good relationship with Billy Ambrose, beginning when we trained together at Bill Cline's gym. Billy was a man of good principles, so I felt I would be able to reason with him.

My decision to pay Billy a visit at the London Hospital was for two reasons. One was out of respect and the other to find out the information I needed to be clued up on how many witnesses were present on the night in question. They would have to be intercepted and asked – or coerced – not to give evidence against the accused, Nash, Reed and Pyle. Just before I entered the hospital ward I carefully looked around the corridor to see who was present. I noticed a woman I recognised as Billy's wife, but thankfully no law. I acknowledged other friends in the room with a nodding gesture as I politely asked Billy's wife for permission to visit her husband for five minutes, to which she agreed.

I was in a bit of a dilemma with the assignment I had undertaken. As I said, I had the utmost respect for Billy Ambrose and he knew it. Being a man of sound principle I felt certain that he wouldn't deviate from our moral code and prosecute Nash and the others. Yet here I was pleading leniency on the accused's behalf to their victim. As it turned out, he didn't take my plea as a personal slight against him and knowing that made my conscience a bit easier.

Jimmy, Joe and John were eventually arrested and charged with murder and the trial was to take place at the Old Bailey. While the trial was pending Ron and I visited Jimmy Nash who was on remand in the hospital section of Brixton Prison. It was normal practice to admit murderers onto the hospital wing. A screw sat close to Jimmy while we spoke and took notes to record the conversation. Jimmy was not at all intimidated or perturbed by the officer's presence and as we continued to speak, he made a noose out of a thread of cotton and dangled it to and fro – Jimmy always did have a bizarre sense of humour and this little joke seemed to please him immensely. I had made a point of meeting all the witnesses to the shooting and invited them to the Double R Club for drinks. As I sat drinking with Jimmy Cooney's girlfriend, she intimated that she would disappear for a while in exchange for a favour. Apparently she had some medical problems and required the immediate services of a good doctor. Fortunately we had an excellent doctor on the firm and a compromise was reached.

During the trial, I sat with Jimmy Nash in the part of the court set aside for the accused's family. Jimmy Nash was found guilty of manslaughter and sentenced to five years imprisonment. Joe Pyle and John Reed were both acquitted.

Ron and I were with the other members of our firm sitting in a gambling club at Wellington Way, Bow, when the news bulletin giving the result was transmitted. We were all ecstatic with the result and raised our glasses to Jimmy, Joe and John. We also toasted the health of Billy Ambrose, who not only refused to testify against the accused, but actually helped them in their defence. Today Billy Ambrose is a highly successful businessman and in the opinion of Ron and me he deserves everything he's got because it couldn't have happened to a nicer fella.

Our manor was home to people of many different backgrounds. To be a foreigner in the London underworld didn't mean you had to have been born outside British shores; there were plenty of other people who felt out of their depth among us. Peter Jenkins, known as the 'Mayfair Playboy', was one such person. He had been convicted of a jewellery robbery in the 1950s that took place in a hotel in the Mayfair area. Jenkins and his accomplice had booked into a Mayfair hotel under false names and then phoned a jeweller and asked the manager to bring a tray of valuable rings to them in a briefcase at a specified time. He took the tray of rings out and displayed them on the table in the hotel room so that they could look and select an engagement ring. When the manager placed the jewellery on the table, they did not hesitate to bludgeon him around his head with coshes until he fell to the floor with blood gushing from his head wounds. They picked up the jewellery, placed the tray in a small case and left the hotel. Sometime later Peter Jenkins was arrested with his colleague and charged with malicious wounding and robbery. They had been spending the proceeds in various nightclubs in such a way that they had drawn attention to themselves.

When Peter Jenkins appeared at the Old Bailey in number one court, the gallery was packed with debutantes and society people. They had come to see their fallen member even though he was disgraced. Jenkins and his co-accused were sentenced to seven years' penal servitude. Peter was sent to Dartmoor Prison to serve his sentence. Ron and I looked after him with tobacco and the odd bottle of Scotch while he was inside and let him know that when he was eventually released he could come and see us at the Double R anytime and we would be pleased to see him. He did turn up and when I greeted him I could not help feeling sorry for him because the sentence had taken its toll on a person whom I had weighed up as a non-criminal type. Despite the fact that he had just come out of prison, it was obvious that criminal society was unnatural and alien to him. The Double R Club was frequented by criminal types as well as straight people and when Peter was in conversation with some of the criminal element, I could see he was like a fish out of water. It was obvious to me that it must have been the same for him when he was in Dartmoor Prison, which must have made his sentence that much more of an ordeal. He was now an alcoholic and all he had left was his educated way of speaking and his gentleman-like ways. I gave Peter Jenkins a few quid and made his evening as comfortable as possible, plying him with drinks. Some years later I read a daily newspaper which had a very small write-up in it that read:

Peter Jenkins, alias the Mayfair Playboy, has been found dead in a lodging house in the area of Bayswater. He died of alcohol poisoning.

It seemed he could not pick up the pieces to start a new life and his conviction banished him from high society. I found Peter Jenkins an interesting but sad victim of life's stage.

Peter Jenkins wasn't the only unlikely character to be found in the East End. Not everyone in the East End of my youth had British heritage – even if this wasn't immediately obvious. Take Albert Dimes, for instance. Albert, whose whose real name was Alberto Dimeo, was a central figure in the Soho area, and yet his connections stretched well beyond the boundaries of the West End. He owned a betting shop there and Henry Cooper, the former Heavyweight Champion of Britain, was often seen in his company, because Albert was a regular fight fan and was present at all the main tournaments. He towered over six foot tall with sleek black hair and elegant, handsome features, all generated by his Italian heritage. He controlled the point-to-point meetings all over the country and always ensured that Ron and I had decent pitches at the courses. Albert was a very likeable person, with a pleasing per-sonality and a tendency to chain-smoke constantly. Ron and I were in his betting shop and hanging on the wall were the gloves that Muhammad Ali and Henry Cooper had worn while fighting each other. They must have been very valuable and treasured possessions but without hesitation he took them down and presented them to us as a gift. One of the last meetings I had with Italian Albert took place in Soho when he and I had a rendezvous with Philadelphia Mafia boss Angelo Bruno. When Angelo Bruno came to London, Ron and I were invited to meet him at the Hilton Hotel. Angelo was very short with a stocky build. At the time of the meeting he wore a beret which covered his bald head, and he wore glasses. We had a cup of coffee with him and he asked questions about London, centred around the gambling scene. Years later Bruno was shot dead, riddled with bullets as he sat in his car.

Ronnie and I often had visitors from overseas at our clubs. Businessmen and villains whose influence was far greater than our own. One evening in 1966 I had a meet with some Americans in the Pigalle Restaurant Club in Regent Street. When I arrived there were four Americans present, two of them I knew and the other two were strangers. These people were men of respect, and I will never forget this particular night, as among this small group was a small-built, dark-skinned man of about seventy years of age. He was obviously Sicilian and it was quite clear to me that his three friends held him in some reverence. At one stage of the conversation someone passed the cigarettes around and I lit my lighter for one of the men who was to my left. As I did so, he said to me in a friendly tone of voice, 'Reg, would you light the cigarette of our friend here first out of respect because he is the elder.' The friend on my left gestured with his hand indicating the Sicilian on my right. This was a lesson in respect I shall never forget. The names of these men will remain unsaid. Throughout the night I learned that the elder man who was held in such reverence was a Don of Dons.

Some of these men of respect were fascinating storytellers, about their own experience. I often used to meet one, called Herb, in a London hotel. We would sit and have a coffee while he told me fascinating tales. Sometimes I would get to the hotel early to join him for breakfast, and he would sit at the table wearing an immaculate white satin dressing gown of short length.

One of the nicest people it has been my pleasure to meet was a man of respect whose first name was Joe. His city was Washington, DC. He was a classy dresser, very mild-mannered, and wore smart tinted glasses. His fingernails were manicured to perfection and he wore expensive jewellery without being ostentatious. Charlie, Ron and I would meet Joe and his charming wife at the Hilton Hotel on regular occasions. He had come up through the ranks and was now recognised as a top man within the family. At one time in his younger days, he had been convicted of knifing a man to death during a back-street dice game.

Another of our visitors was Tony 'Ducks' Carrillo. He is now serving a hundred years in a prison somewhere in America after being convicted of extortion. Tony was born in

Brooklyn and was the main man in the garment industry. Tony was short and very thick-set, had a broken nose and a strong Brooklyn accent and while he came across as a good person, at the same time he was not someone to mess with. During the mid-1950s he came to London and stayed in a flat in the Bayswater area where he asked us to visit him so we could talk of things in general. They had also invited Tony Mulla to join them, but Tony did not show up and Tony Carrillo was not at all happy with him for this lack of respect. We were invited to go and see Tony Carrillo and be his guests in Brooklyn whenever we wanted to and he said he would show us around New York. Much to my regret we did not make the journey, though Ron did go to New York years later.

There was among these people one by the name of Skinny who lived in an old precinct building in New York. Others told me that although he was very frail in build he really used to put the fear into people. At one time there was a world heavyweight fight champion who had not carried out instructions he had been given by the family. He was invited for a talk with Skinny in his car. They drove around the block a couple of times and what was said isn't known but when the boxer finally got out of the car he was shaking so much that he could hardly stand. I relate this story to show that men of violence come in all shapes and sizes and are not necessarily big men physically.

Little Joe was from New York and when he passed away

recently all the men of respect were genuinely sad. Joe was born without a cent, and had risen through the ranks to become a man of respect and wealth. He always remembered his days of hunger and would give precious gifts freely to his friends. Just a few years ago my brother Ron received a beautiful gold ring with diamonds, which Joe had sent to him at Broadmoor all the way from New York. He still wears it today.

Eddie the Sicilian was another man of respect Ron and I were lucky enough to encounter. He had contacts all over the world in gambling, show business and fights. Eddie visited London in the mid-1960s and during that time Charlie, Ron and I made him welcome as our guest. He stayed in one of the best hotels in London and we would meet in his room before taking him on a tour of the city for late drinking sessions. There was a large radiogram in his room and he insisted on keeping it on while we discussed business so that the music would drown out any conversation if the room was bugged. Perhaps his paranoia was founded as Eddie was shot dead by two hit men in New York in his forties.

In the 1960s there was a connected family in Brooklyn, who had become infamous over the years and were portrayed as the gangsters of that era. They were the Gallo family, led by Crazy Joe Gallo and his brothers Larry and Al. Crazy Joe had become a legend because of his wild exploits and behaviour. He had been kicked out of the army, having been classified as a psychopath, which perhaps went some way to explaining his nickname. He also kept a tiger in a cage in the basement of his house and if he was upset with anyone he would show them the tiger and threaten to chuck them in the cage. At one time Crazy Joe heard that Billy Daniels, the singer who had made the song 'That Old Black Magic' famous, had been dating one of his girlfriends, a good-looking air hostess. He had taken Billy to see the ferocious tiger and it was said that forever after Billy Daniels never looked at an air hostess again, other than to order a quick gin and tonic.

Larry and Al Gallo were also more than capable when it came to handling problems and people, but were considered mild in comparison with their brother Joe. Crazy Joe was eventually shot dead while dining in a restaurant in the area of Little Italy in New York, but he had managed to follow the three hit men as far as the pavement outside the restaurant before he collapsed and died in the gutter.

When Ron first went to New York, he and Joe Kaufman went to a small café situated in the Little Italy area. Outside the café they were met by Edmondo, who was a dwarf and a mascot of the Gallo family, and their friend Tony 'Punchie' Illiano. My brother Ron, who had no fear of people or situations, had gone to the café to seek out and introduce himself to Crazy Joe and his brothers. Edmondo showed Ron and Joe Kaufman inside and asked them to sit down at a table and wait while he went into the kitchen area of the café to make a phone call. A few minutes later a group of people encircled Ron and Joe Kaufman, and one of these was Punchie Illiano. He asked Ron and Joe a few questions so he could check out their credentials. Eventually, after Punchie had checked them out, Al Gallo arrived on the scene and met Ron and Joe. Ron was told that Crazy Joe was not available, he was away on business and Larry Gallo was in hospital dying of cancer. Ron arranged, as a sign of respect, to send Larry a basket of fruit. On his return, Ron made plans for Tony to be our guest in London, but this never came about because a little while after this Ron and I were sentenced to life imprisonment.

The legal system actually broadened our horizons at times, of course. In the year 1959 I had just been sentenced to eighteen months in prison for demanding money with menaces – this despite the fact that I was completely innocent of the charge. I was sitting on a wooden bench below the court of the Old Bailey when the screws opened the door and escorted in a man who had also just been convicted. He introduced himself to me as Carmelo Messina, of the infamous Messina family. He was short in height, swarthy, and was very polite. His birthplace was Malta and Carmelo and his brothers were well known for running a call-girl racket in central London during the 1950s. The family became multi-millionaires through this. Carmelo told me that on his conviction he was innocent, and the police from West End Central Police Station had convinced a prostitute to give false evidence against him, saying that she paid Carmelo from her immoral earnings, and on her word alone he had been sentenced to four years' imprisonment. I couldn't take his protestation of innocence very seriously as the family business was an open secret, but I could sympathise with the method used to catch him. He was an interesting person and when we arrived at Wandsworth prison I asked a few people to watch out for him, because though I disliked ponces I looked upon Carmelo in a different light. He told me that living off the earnings of a woman was not considered immoral in his home country of Malta. Whichever way one looked at the Messina family, they were professional in the way they chose to make a living.

Many years later, around 1967, Ron and I received a message from Carmelo saying if we could travel to Malta, he and his family had a proposition to put to us. This showed me that he had not forgotten my presence in those dreary days spent in Wandsworth. Ron and I never made the trip because some time later we were arrested, which led to my present predicament. The Messina name has a place in the annals of professional crime, and a place in my memory of the colourful 1950s and 1960s, and today I still wonder what proposition Carmelo and his family had in mind.

9

Local Legends

Living as they did in one of London's worst areas, East End men were tough, hard and took no nonsense from anyone, particularly authority. Ronnie and I grew up among such people. You either fought or you went under, and my family was no different. My grandfathers on both sides were tough fighting men and I've even seen Grandma Lee up-end a man for treating her with disrespect. Uncle Joe was no villain but he could have a fight when necessary and even went up against the Sabini mob in his younger days. Our father wasn't a fighter but he carried a distain for authority all his life, something that rubbed off on his boys. Our lives were populated with villains and those on the edge of villainy. It was the norm rather than the exception.

I feel as though I have been fortunate in having been acquainted with this breed of men, almost all of them villains, whose like will never be seen again, because the East End has changed beyond recognition. No longer a breeding ground for poverty and disease, and now populated by a much more cosmopolitan crowd, it is completely different from the East End I grew up in. Though they lived on the wrong side of the law, those villains were as much part of the history of London as those whose fame is remembered in other areas. A record of these men, as I remember them, might help to paint a picture of the London scene during the 1950s and 60s. London was originally a collection of small villages that over the years became joined together. What remained though was the individuality of these areas and each had its guv'nor, hard men who ruled their manors with fists, knives and guns.

When I was in my twenties the man I wanted to emulate most of all was the former boss of London's underworld, Billy Hill. The prime reason for my admiration, apart from his ability to be very violent when necessary, was that he had a sharp and quick thinking mind that appealed to me. It was just as well we didn't go up against him in the incident I mentioned earlier, as Ron and I became friends with him and we were to learn a great deal about putting thoughts into action simply by observing how he handled different situations. One example concerns the time when Ron and myself,

Charlie and a mutual friend, Willie Malone, were at Vallance Road. The telephone rang and Ron took the call. It was Billy Hill and he said, 'Ron, will you come over to my flat as soon as possible.' Ron replied, 'OK, we're on our way.' We each collected a gun from the bedroom, jumped in the motor outside and drove to Bill's flat in Moscow Road, Bayswater. Arriving in less than fifteen minutes, we knocked and were invited in. I said to Billy, 'What's the trouble, we've brought some shooters.' He just laughed and said, 'Hang on there for a minute,' and went into the bedroom. When he came back he tossed a bundle containing five hundred pounds of brand new banknotes onto the table. 'Take that few quid for your trouble and cut it up between you. I was only testing you to see how fast you'd get over here, or if you'd blank the emergency.' This is just one instance of his great sense of humour and of his good thinking.

Another time, two fellas and I went to the 21 Rooms in the West End. The 21 Rooms was owned by the Meadow brothers and was one of the most exclusive clubs in London at the time. I believe it got its name from having twenty-one bedrooms. On this occasion we were refused admittance by the two doormen dressed in tuxedos. I struck one of them on the chin, and as he hit the deck, my two friends applied the same treatment to his partner, who quickly joined him on the floor. I immediately thought we'd be arrested for grievous bodily harm, due to the fact that one of the doormen may have recognised me. I also knew that Billy Hill procured a nice few quid out of the 21 so this sort of thing didn't happen. Even though it was the early hours I decided that the best thing to do was to see Billy, confess and explain the situation. He was at home when we arrived and invited us in. I gave him my version of what had happened and asked him if he could find out if any charges were going to be brought against us. To my surprise, Billy was not the slightest bit perturbed that we had floored the doormen at the club. In fact his reaction was quite the opposite. He telephoned the owner of the club and said, 'This is Billy, I hear you've just had some trouble, so I'm ringing to let you know I've taken care of it. Leave everything to me.' Ending his telephone conversation, Bill replaced the receiver and seemed very pleased with himself. He took a roll of notes out of his pocket, handed me £300 and said, 'Take that few quid. It would have cost me a lot more to have arranged such a commotion to ensure my services are still necessary.' The point he was making was that he had turned disadvantage to advantage and the next day he would probably receive five grand from the owners for preventing any further incidents. The probability of this seemed highly unlikely as such an exclusive establishment didn't attract much trouble. Still, three tough guys from the East End had presented Billy with just the opportunity he needed to extort a few more quid out of the Meadows brothers. This was a classic example of how Billy could weigh up a situation and turn it to his advantage. He was respected all over London and one of his favourite haunts was an area called

Warren Street where he used to associate with all the car dealers.

One time in his younger days, Billy visited Johannesburg in South Africa, along with Bobby Ramsey, the ex-fighter. They were in a club one night and while Billy gambled, Ramsey watched. An argument started between Billy and the minder of the club, an ex-professional wrestler. The minder placed his hands on Billy's shoulders to throw him out, whereupon Billy drew a knife and cut him up so badly he needed a hundred stitches. Outside the club Billy produced a revolver and aimlessly fired pot shots at one of the other guards. Ramsey was arrested for this offence and served three months in a South African jail, while Billy evaded capture and escaped back to London.

Ron and me, in the company of Ian Barrie and Christine Boyce, whom I spent lot of time with in those days, went to Tangiers and were made very welcome by Billy. We had gone there because we found out that the law was making itself very busy and was out to arrest us for the murder of George Cornell and other crimes. We had left England in a small six-seater plane from the area of Hastings, stopped off in France, and from there we went on to Tangiers. Billy Hill was a great host and would tell us of his exploits with the criminal fraternity. He told us of a big robbery he was involved in in Eastcastle Street where after hijacking a Post Office van, he and others had got away with quarter of a million in cash. This robbery made headlines for the week and the law didn't have a clue who had pulled it off. After lying low for a few days Billy decided to move the cash to another safe house. He put the sacks in the boot, headed away from his Bayswater flat and broke down about a mile away. He got out of the car and seeing a policeman on point duty asked him to push it while Billy sat behind the wheel. The car eventually started and after profusely thanking the policeman, he drove to Spitalfields Market to meet Slip Sullivan who was waiting with a lorry laden with sacks of potatoes. They placed the quarter mill underneath the potatoes on the back of the open lorry, and then took turns to watch the load discreetly to make sure their hard-earned money was not stolen. Billy and Slip were both pulled in for the robbery, but were released after being questioned because they had a watertight alibi for the time of the robbery. Later on in life, Slip Sullivan was stabbed to death by the woman he was sleeping with. It was ironic that he should be killed by a friend after surviving so many battles with villains in the underworld.

Billy Hill was not only someone who taught us how to handle our business better but he introduced us to many people who would become very useful later on. One day Billy Hill phoned Ron and me and asked if we'd meet him at Pat Kennedy's pub, the Star in Belgrave Square, Knightsbridge. He wanted us to meet Charles Da Silva. When we reached the pub Billy ordered drinks and introduced us to Da Silva. Then he told us that Charlie Mitchell had been taking liberties with Da Silva by blagging money off him. He added that Da Silva would rather pay Ron and me money regularly rather than let Mitchell blag him, so would we mind him? We agreed and shook hands to bind the deal. We chatted for an hour or so and then left the pub, but not before we had agreed to meet Charles the following day at one of London's best hotels where he had a full suite. He always lived in style and was booked into the hotel as a sheikh.

Charles was born in Indonesia and had a tanned complexion, jet-black hair, perfect white teeth, and good looks in general. He wore just enough jewellery and was a perfect dresser. He was known in criminal circles as 'The King of the Con Men', and when he conned someone it was always for an enormous sum of money. After we met up with him he gave us a considerable sum of money that would set the future pattern for a regular income for looking after him. Charles came from a wealthy family and was used to high living. He told us that he could have been wealthy by working in his family's business, but preferred the excitement and buzz of pulling off a big con. He would only ever drive a Rolls-Royce or a Bentley and only dine in the most exclusive hotels.

A little while later Charles was arrested for selling a fleet of yachts to a couple of mugs for somewhere in the region of one million pounds. The yachts, as to be expected, were non-existent. He was given bail and sent for trial. While awaiting trial he continued to enjoy his luxurious lifestyle, but one night, just before it began, he went to an exclusive hotel, booked a suite of rooms, ordered a bottle of brandy and took an overdose of tablets. He left a suicide note saying he couldn't face any more prison time and asked his family to forgive him.

To me, Billy Hill was the epitome of what a professional criminal should be. He was not heavily built, but with a knife he could be lethal. He was a smart dresser, a good host, and the best of spenders. He was born into a criminal family and his early years were spent carrying out burglaries. Later on he teamed up with Jack Comer, who was known as Spotty, for ventures into the black market and protection racketeering in the West End. Jack liked to think the Spotty nickname came from the fact that he was always on the spot, but the truth is it came from the black mole on his face. Convicted of robbing a warehouse, Billy got the only prison term he would ever serve. Moving into smuggling from Morocco, where he had bought his wife Gypsy the biggest nightclub in the area, he ended up as a property developer. He retired from crime and his other ventures in 1974 and died in 1984. In his last days he became pretty much a recluse, dying a millionaire at the age of seventy-three. In many ways I like to think that I have come close to emulating him, though to be honest, I acknowledge that he stands alone and there will never be another like him. I could say he was our mentor and taught us much of what would stand us in good stead in our rising future.

Jack Spot, the former Jewish boss of London, was another

London figure Ron and I came up against in our career. Born at Aldgate, east London, in the early 1930s and christened Jacob Colmore, today he must be around seventy-six years of age. In his younger days he was a powerful figure of a man, with looks and features synonymous with Al Capone. He was very clean-living and abstained from taking alcohol or cigarettes, but he'd take the occasional cigar. Though he was very affluent, one of Jack's bad points was that he tended to be rather mean and was not a liberal spender. Still, his fascinating personality cancelled out his frugality. Initially Ron and I got to know him well in our early twenties when he gave us pitches at the races. In the early 1950s when I was around twenty-one, I travelled up to Manchester with Jack, accompanied by George and Jimmy Woods. Spot had arranged a meeting with the owner of a raincoat factory and from this meeting he came away four grand richer. On the train journey back to London, he handed me twenty-five pounds. As a novice to the business I accepted this paltry sum with some indignation, but held my tongue. Many years later Jack opened a club in the West End and for business reasons I arranged for someone to set fire to it, the result being that it burnt to the ground. Despite this course of action, I still retained a fond memory of Jack's significant role during those early years.

In the 1950s when Spot and Albert Dimes had a knife fight in Frith Street, central Soho, both men received knife wounds, but Spot had severe lacerations down the right side of his face. They were arrested, charged with causing an affray and sent to trial. Two famous hearings resulted from this case but each time the jury found Spot and Dimes innocent and acquitted them, regardless of the fact that both were cut to pieces. The entire episode was consequently known as the fight that never was.

It was through Jack Spot's firm that Ron and I first became friends with Geoff Allen over thirty-five years ago. It is a strange but interesting story of how our paths crossed, led to our friendship, and brought Geoff into our family as a considered uncle. One particular night Ron and I were sitting in the Vienna Rooms drinking coffee, enjoying the social banter, when Moishe Blueboy, a recognised villain in Jack Spot's firm, came over and put a proposition to us. 'Do you fancy a ride in the country? I've found a mug farmer that I am going to take a few quid off in a bent game of cards. He lives near Stansted Airport so if you want to come for the ride I'll square you up a few quid when I've taken his money.' Blueboy, incidentally, was one of the best shady card players in the country, so in anticipation of earning a bit of easy money, we accepted his invitation. Accompanying us were Sammy Lederman and Johnny Stracey, both West End characters. John drove us to Bishop's Stortford and eventually we pulled up outside a quaint little cottage. Geoff invited us in and without any messing about, broke open a fresh pack of cards and suggested him and Moishe should play gin rummy. Ron and I watched closely as the inscrutable Blueboy flawlessly dealt the cards. All this was good experience and I tried to remember every action and reaction of the two players for future reference. When Geoff left the room, Blueboy would wink at us just to let us know that he still had control over the game and would 'soon take the sucker for a nice few quid'. They played continuously until the small hours, then called it a day. Blueboy, true to his words, had come up trumps and fiddled Geoff Allen out of eleven hundred pounds, a substantial amount in those days. Geoff seemed to accept defeat graciously but said to Moishe that he would be unable to pay his debt until the bank opened at ten o'clock. So he suggested the best thing to do was for us to wait for him at the White Hart Inn in the centre of the village, and he'd meet us there at eleven o'clock. We were all jubilant at the thought of our good fortune and on reaching the hotel ordered a celebration breakfast to toast our success. Watching the clock, we anxiously awaited the arrival of Geoff Allen. Time seemed to stand still, especially when eleven o'clock came and went and the man didn't show. None of us were unduly suspicious of his delay but as time went on Moishe decided to give him a call to find out what the problem was. He eventually answered the phone. As we watched Blueboy, it was obvious something was wrong by the expression on his face. He replaced the receiver as though it were a lifeline and he was suffering a cardiac arrest. Geoff Allen had told Blueboy, in no uncertain terms, that he had no intention of paying up and if any attempt was made to go near the cottage, he was waiting with a shotgun and wouldn't hesitate to use it. Blueboy actually looked quite ill at the prospect of losing all his hard-earned cash, but what could we do except accept the situation and return home empty-handed. I have to say Moishe was an excellent paymaster, and had the venture been successful, Ron and I would have been well rewarded. Sad to say Blueboy has since passed away, but I'll wager you wherever he is, be it up or down, he'll be scheming to earn himself a few quid.

The Geoff Allen affair did have a happy ending as, using Billy Hill's advice, I decided to turn disadvantage to advantage and contact the man again. A few weeks later I caught a train to Bishop's Stortford. I knocked on the door and when Geoff answered he looked at me and said, 'You've got some nerve coming here but come in, we might be able to discuss some future business.' I did just that and it proved a very lucrative deal for both of us in the future. He eventually became a big property dealer and Ron and I were often privileged to be guests in his palatial mansion right up until we were imprisoned.

Another man we were privileged to befriend was John Nash. About the same age as Ron and me, he originates from the Angel, Islington, and we have known him since we were sixteen. We first met in Shepton Mallet Prison, where all three of us were serving a term of army imprisonment. John was one of the best fighting men in the London area and had the physique of an athlete and the looks and high cheekbones of the actor Jack Palance. One of seven brothers, John and his family used to look after the Bagatelle Club in the West End, another favourite haunt among villains. John is also credited with having played a dominant role over the years in the changing scene of underworld politics in the capital.

I was in Wandsworth Prison with him when he was serving two years for possessing a gun. He told me he had been fitted up on this charge and I have every reason to believe him, though it was no secret that John's nickname of 'Peacemaker' came not only from his negotiating skills between rival gangs but because he invariably carried a Colt Peacemaker, the original Wild West gun.

Johnny is a compulsive gambler and I recall one evening, when he was playing in a West End casino, an ex-wrestler tried to take a liberty with him, So John picked up a chair and smashed it over the fella's head leaving him with little inclination to wrestle anyone again.

On the other side of the coin were men like Tommy Venables. Tommy lived in Menotti Street, near Vallance Road. He was about five foot eight inches tall with blue eyes and one of the worst razor slashes I have ever seen down the right-hand side of his face. He was a villain and a con man and had never done an honest day's work in his life. Tommy taught us many tricks which came in handy when we became con artists ourselves.

Tommy would always be on the lookout for a likely client as a receiver of stolen goods and work on him what is known as the 'comer'. He would offer to sell him a lorryload of cigarettes and would arrange a meeting place to drop the load. His driver would deliver the goods and the receiver would climb into the back of the lorry to inspect the merchandise. He would open one of the top cartons and take out a sample, then Tommy would give him the hurry-up, suggesting the possibility that the law might be in the area. Invariably the receiver would hastily hand over the cash and speedily unload his consignment of stolen cigarettes in anticipation of the police arriving. Before the last box was off the lorry, Tommy would be in his local putting himself outside of a couple of large Scotches. It would only be when the dealer went to resell the load at a later date that he'd discover to his amazement that he had been duped and the boxes contained not packs of cigarettes but sawdust. The fact that Tommy was well known as a villain would usually ensure that the injured party did not go to the police or seek recompense.

A favourite con trick that Tommy used, as did many others in the East End, myself included, was to go to the main dealer in snide rings, Red-Faced Tommy. He would give us the rings on credit with an understanding that we would look after him when a mug was found to buy one of the fake rings. Tommy Venables sold so many of these rings all over London he was lucky to have only one scar down his face, because many receivers had a heavy on the firm to sort out anyone who targeted them as suckers.

East End villains needed a lot of bottle to work as they did.

Albert the Jar, so named because he sold so many jargoons, or fake stones, would laugh his way out of any situation if any receiver caught up with him after being taken for a ride. Once he had their money, the suckers had no chance of retrieving it. But Albert was an amiable fella and could charm his way out of any predicament others would regard as highly dangerous. His eyes would really sparkle after he'd got a result from conning someone out of a few notes. He had the con man's silver tongue. I have often seen him drinking and cracking jokes with someone he had duped, and you could guarantee before they parted Albert would have smoothed over any unpleasant atmosphere between them. He would say, 'There's my phone number, find me a customer for one of my jargoons and I'll cut you in for a few quid.' The sucker would be so eager to get his money back that he would go along with Albert's scheme and feel quite pleased that he was going to be compensated. They would shake hands and part amicably.

But this lifestyle eventually started to take its toll. One day Albert was feeling under the weather so he decided to visit our crooked doctor for some advice. Whatever was wrong with Albert I can assure you that it wasn't his conscience playing him up because he used to say to me, 'Reggie, when you find a mug squeeze him like a lemon then leave him screaming. There's one walking over London Bridge every day.' Anyway, Albert saw the doctor and said, 'For some reason or other, Doc, my nerves are all shot up.' To which the doctor replied, 'It's no wonder. I'm surprised you've never had a nervous breakdown. You go conning people left, right and centre, never knowing when one of them might take a knife to you. You accept it as the norm to drink with these people, laughing and joking after you've ripped them off, but I'm surprised you've never been found in a river or alleyway dead.' Albert told me this story one day while we were drinking in the Double R Club. Always one with a great sense of humour, he seemed genuinely sorry for himself and said to me, 'Those who work in factories for a living don't know what peace of mind they've got.' Needless to say Albert the Jar was one of my best customers at the Double R.

Albert wasn't the only one to suffer terribly under the stress of the East End. John Hall, an East End gunman, came to a bad end himself. John had been arrested and placed in the cells on many occasions over the years, triggering off a claustrophobia condition. These attacks became more severe each time and consequently his hatred towards the law increased. One day he was called into a police station for questioning. He was lucky this time and was released without charge for the time being. But back at home John began brooding over the threat of further imprisonment and in his confused state of mind decided he had only one course of action. The following day, he walked into a police station, pulled out a revolver and shot dead the first policeman he saw before turning around and walking out. He then went to a phone booth where he paused to make a call. A short time later, shots were heard and John Hall lay dead with a bullet in his brain. The police reported suicide but local opinion disputed the allegation.

For some in the East End, prison was just a different way of life. Charlie Richardson and his brother Eddie, both from south London, were infamous as leaders of the 'Richardson Torture Gang'. Charlie and Eddie were eventually convicted of fraud, extortion, assault and grievous bodily harm. They were sentenced to twenty-five and ten years, respectively. Ron and I first encountered Charlie Richardson in the army prison at Shepton Mallet, where we were all serving sentences. I later served time with Eddie Richardson at Leicester Prison in 1971. We were both in the security block and passed the time by playing table tennis together, while the tabloid newspapers still reported the feuding rivalry between the Kray and Richardson gangs. Years later, I met up with Charlie again at Parkhurst and his sense of humour, which always appealed to me, had not been lost. When he finished work for the day in the prison workshop, he sought the comfort of his favourite armchair, refusing to move for anyone or anything. He even delegated someone to make him tea and was content to sit there until it was time for him to be locked up in the seclusion of his cell.

Frankie Fraser is now a retired con after having spent over twenty years in prison. He acquired the alias 'Mad Frank' due to his time spent in Broadmoor. Since his teenage days he has been a force to be reckoned with in the criminal underworld and until his retirement he remained one of the top men in the London scene. He received a fifteen-year sentence for his part in the famous Richardson trials and seven years for his involvement in the Jack Spot attack.

It's funny how times change, but if I met them today I'd buy Charlie or Frankie a drink. It doesn't matter what the connection was, as we grow older we miss those people we knew in our youth, probably because they were such a significant part of our past. In those days there was a tendency to lose ourselves in complacency and simply allow ourselves to flow along with the tide of time, not realising until we looked back that we had drifted further than we anticipated and our lives were drowning in dreams and memories.

Occasionally a friend would become an enemy, of course. George Dixon from West Ham was six foot tall with blond hair and his physique was complemented by extremely broad shoulders. He was an accomplished fighter and had knocked out many rivals with a single punch. His brother Alan was an equally tough street-fighter and often the two would fight each other as furiously as they fought others. Both have marked faces from the many battles they were in during the 1950s and early 60s, but George and Alan are today smartly dressed and handsome men.

At one time George was in the Rising Sun public house in Roman Road, when, in full view of everyone, a fella accosted him with a sawn-off shotgun. George calmly pushed the weapon aside, floored the fella with one punch and claimed the weapon. Big George, as he was fondly called, has been hit on the head, had his face slashed, been shot at and served time in prison – yet still he survived.

When we were all free men though, Ron and George had a disagreement and as such George had been warned to stay out of the Regency gambling club. But George, being the man he was, disobeyed Ron's advice and entered with two friends. I watched Ron's reaction: his face went white with anger. He eased himself from the chair he was sitting in and headed for the men's room where I knew he kept a revolver hidden in the top of the cistern. Presently he entered the casino area and stared at Dixon, then almost nonchalantly, he pulled the gun out of his pocket and calmly raised it in the air, lining it up with the intention of shooting Dixon in the head. Acting on impulse, I grabbed the gun handle and caused it to fall to the floor. As it came to rest I heard a click and shouted out a warning to Dixon, 'Fuck off quick.' George grasped the situation he was in and he and his companions legged it out of the club.

Ron and me then had an argument as to why I had interfered in his personal business. Later on though, when he opened the gun we saw the firing pin had put an indentation in the bullet, but for some reason it hadn't gone off. Sometime later when they had patched up their differences, Ron presented George with the bullet to keep as a souvenir and I heard that George wore it around his neck for many years.

When Ron and I were convicted in 1969, the police concentrated their efforts on securing another conviction against George and Alan. They suggested the Dixons were trying to fill the void left by us in the local underground scene. They were convicted and sent down for twelve and nine years respectively.

I made many mistakes and misjudgements over the years and one of these was springing Frank 'The Mad Axeman' Mitchell from Dartmoor, where he was serving a life sentence for holding an old couple captive while he sat over them holding an axe balanced on his knee. Ron and I had met Frank years before when we did time together in Wandsworth. He was a big, powerful man whom no one could control, mainly because he had the mind of a child and like a child if he didn't get his own way he'd kick off, and with someone of his size that caused many problems for the authorities, so much so that they shoved him into Broadmoor and Rampton on a few occasions. But he was a likeable fella in a childish sort of way.

After we'd done our time in Wandsworth, which had only been six months for GBH, Ronnie kept in touch with Frank or, more to the point, Frank kept in touch with Ronnie. Letter after letter arrived at Vallance Road and because Ronnie was no letter writer most of the time it was Mum who answered them. They were all mostly in the same vein with Frank complaining that the Home Office would not give him a release date, which all prisoners want because it gives them something to work towards. Eventually Ronnie got it into his head that it would be doing Frank a big favour if we got him out of Dartmoor. At one time, if you were a mental patient and got out of the hospital and stayed at large for some time without getting into trouble the authorities that had put you there had to reconsider your position. I am sure this was in the back of Ronnie's mind though the same does not apply to a prisoner on the run. But at the same time he thought a bit of publicity might force the prison authorities to give Frank a date when he could hope to be released. Why I let myself get talked into it I don't know, but when Ronnie got a bee in his bonnet he could be very persuasive. I came round in the end, thinking if nothing else it would stick two fingers up to the law, which we'd been doing since we were kids.

Getting out of Dartmoor was not quite accurate because most of Frank's days were spent outside the walls anyway. It seemed the screws found him a lot easier to control if he was left to his own devices and that meant allowing him to wander around on the moor and even pop into a local pub with a screw keeping an eye on him. So lifting him would be no problem.

To set the plan in action I got the old-time boxer Ted 'Kid' Lewis to offer to go into the prison and give a talk while showing boxing films. The governor loved the idea and of course I stuck a hat on and a pair of heavy glasses and accompanied Ted in disguise. This gave me a chance to have a word with Frank and fill him in on what we planned. A week later I sent Albert Donoghue, 'Mad' Teddy Smith and Billy Exley to pick Frank up at a prearranged location. It was as simple as that and in no time, even before he was reported missing, he was safely inside the flat of Lennie Dunn in Canning Town.

Apart from Ron and me being pretty busy we'd heard that Frank was making a fucking nuisance of himself so we didn't go round to see him. We'd done what we'd set out to do and as far as we were concerned that was that. We heard he wanted to go up West to find himself a girl and we couldn't let that happen because without a shadow of a doubt, being as conspicuous as he was, he'd have been picked up in five minutes. So we arranged for one of our girls from the Winston Club, Lisa Prescott, to go round to the flat and keep him company. That kept him quiet for a while but then he started complaining he wasn't being shown respect because we weren't spending time with him and he was bored in the flat. More and more he was threatening to come to Vallance Road to find us.

We had three choices. Hand him over to the police, in which case he would point the finger at us straight away. Just let him leave, whereupon he'd be lifted very soon and again put us in the frame or, the third option, which really was the only solution to our problem before it all went pear-shaped, we'd have him killed. With the idea in place we didn't hang about because even Scotch Jack Dickson was having a problem keeping him under control and he was no pushover. I got in touch with Alfie Gerard and another couple of the chaps who would sort out Frank. Alfie and his son Nicki were known throughout the underworld as murder for hire and it was to Nicki that Ronnie Knight turned when he wanted rough justice against the man who had stabbed his younger brother David to death in a club. Nicki did the business for one thousand pounds paid to him by Ronnie but later on was himself shot dead.

Frank was told that he was going to be taken into the country where he would meet up with Ronnie. For a while he was quite happy with the thought of getting out of the flat, but then he kicked up and said he wouldn't go unless Lisa went with him. He was told that that would not be a problem but she would have to travel in a separate motor just in case. He accepted that and couldn't wait for the off. It was dark and raining when Scotch Jack led him downstairs to the waiting van. He opened up the back doors and Frank settled himself on a box that was in the back. Before the van drew away, Alfie and his accomplice pulled their guns out and shot him to death. A tough guy until the end, they had to shoot him more than ten times before he finally slumped to the floor. His body was taken to a farm in Essex and that was the last anyone ever saw of him. Soon after Alfie took off to Australia and the law never followed him even though his name popped into the frame.

*

With twenty-six years behind the door to contemplate the consequences, I can say that what happened to Jack McVitie was a serious lack of judgement. Not that this was the only thing that put me in my present predicament, but it was certainly the catalyst. I hear talk that I was egged on to do what I did by Ronnie, supposedly saying, 'I've done one, now it's your turn.' This was not the case at all. What happened was a very spur-of-the-moment thing and was really brought about by Jack himself.

There was a time when Jack was not a bad bloke. I first met him while serving a sentence, and in the same prison was George Cornell – both men would eventually shape the future of Ronnie and me. I met up with Jack some years later when he came to the Regal looking for work. We gave him some bits and pieces and he carried them out quite satisfactorily, but as time went on he began to drink heavily and was sniffing the white powder. While he was sober and not out of his head he was OK but when not, he turned into big trouble. We had paid him to carry out a job – fifteen hundred pounds, a lot of money back then – but he never saw it through and kept the money. That gave us the hump in itself. Then he started to cause trouble wherever he went and we were getting complaints from club owners who were under our protection.

Both Ronnie and I gave him warning after warning about his behaviour but he never took any notice, so something had to be done. There was a party at Blonde Carol's in Evering

Road and Ronnie decided he would make a final attempt to straighten Jack out, so it was arranged for him to be invited to the party. He turned up very drunk and belligerent from the start. By now Ronnie, whose moods and plans could change in a moment, had decided he didn't want to talk to him and told him to fuck off out of it in no uncertain terms. This didn't please Jack, who stormed around the room shouting, 'You can't fuckinwell treat me like this,' all the while punching his fist into his open palm. When he smashed his fist through a window I'd had enough. I pulled a gun out and aimed it at his head. It didn't fire. I made another attempt and the same thing happened, so with Jack by now throwing punches I picked a knife off the table and stabbed him two or three times until he was lying still on the floor. He'd had every opportunity to leave the party but such was the man he would not be told what to do. If he'd gone when Ronnie ordered him to that episode in my life would never have happened and perhaps I wouldn't be where I am today.

Ronnie and I left immediately and the last thing I remember is seeing Chris Lambrianou crying at the top of the stairs. Brother Charlie, who was in bed at the time of the killing, had nothing whatsoever to do with what happened other than that he came round after we telephoned him in a panic. We often fell back on Charlie as the voice of reason when things got a bit out of hand and he paid a heavy price for trying to help his brothers. Charlie served seven years and the Lambrianou brothers, Chris and Tony, were both sentenced to fifteen years. Another friend, Freddie Foreman, whose drinking club in the Old Kent Road I was a frequent patron of, was convicted of being an accessory after the fact to murder and received ten years. Both brother Charlie and Freddie were convicted on the evidence of Ronald Hart. Later on Freddie was in Leicester Prison at the same time as Eddie Richardson and me, and we all trained together in the gym.

This one incident was to bring our lives tumbling down like a pack of cards. Whether we'd have been pursued by the law quite so strongly if it wasn't for Jack I don't know, but shortly afterwards everything began to unravel and we were arrested. Little did I imagine at the time that twenty-six years later I'd still be locked up and writing about the incident that brought it all about. I've no regrets about killing Jack the Hat because he was the most vexatious person I'd come across in many years. I do regret that perhaps with a bit of forethought it need never have happened, but in the heat of the moment everything goes out of the window.

10

Banged Up

When we were arrested in 1968, many of our so-called friends gave evidence against us at our trial. Once we were convicted and sentenced to thirty years' imprisonment, it seemed as though we had ceased to exist. Every week we looked for letters or some other form of contact from people we had known for years, but nothing came and eventually we gave up and accepted that out of sight meant out of mind, even to close, trusted and respected friends. It was a long time before we found out that the Regional Crime Squad had threatened all those, other than family, that if they continued to support us they could end up in prison themselves. Big Tommy Brown, our old friend 'The Bear', was one of those people, and that great man was to die still hurting from the thought that he had let us down. Only recently I received a letter from an old friend who had not been in touch in all the years I had been away. He asked for my forgiveness and explained the by now familiar story. Watched and threatened, he had been forced to give up trying to contact me and had only just realised that those restrictions had been lifted. Of course I forgave him, as I did all the others, it was out of their hands and I understood. What this does show is how despicable the law can be. Our sentences weren't enough: it had to ostracise Ron and me by blackmailing our supporters. It's no wonder it's despised by many people when such underhand methods are used.

For seventeen and a half years I was classed as a Category A prisoner and held in high-risk security. This meant I never moved anywhere within the prison without being escorted by two screws and Alsatian guard dogs. A pink light bulb would be left shining in my cell all night so that the screws could watch my every movement, like I was a goldfish in a bowl. Cat. A also meant that my visitors, who were few, had to submit three photographs of themselves to the authorities, one of which would be filed with the Home Office. The police would also visit the intended visitor at home to question and vet them. If they had a criminal record their application would be refused. These rules even applied to my parents. Lord Mountbatten introduced this action, and at first myself and other prisoners went on hunger strike against these stringent regulations, but it was to no avail. Cat. A rules still apply today throughout the prison system, and in my opinion they are not necessary beyond four walls. They create a prison within a prison. With the exception of Harry Roberts, who received thirty years in 1966 for shooting three policemen, I spent longer than anyone else in this category. It's a double punishment, created to make communication difficult between the prisoner and his visitors, rather than the prevention of escapes.

I have seen many changes in the system over the years and the most welcome has been the quality of food. Years ago it was hardly fit to eat and came in a three-tier tin that held the whole meal. You ate what you were given or went hungry. Either way, there never seemed to be enough. Today we have more choice and the quality has improved considerably. I could still find room for complaint, but when I think of the starving millions throughout the world, I give thanks for what I have and hold my tongue. But it has always baffled me why prisoners in England are not allowed to receive food parcels from outside, yet in Northern Ireland they can receive as many as their friends care to send in.

Entertainment is another area where things have changed. Today we have music centres, radios, cassette players, and have communal television. Back in 1959 when I was in Wandsworth, you were not allowed a radio until you had served four years of your sentence. At weekends we would have music played from a central radio and piped to loud-speakers on each wing, but we had no choice in what we had to listen to. Still, prisoners are resourceful if nothing else and there was a good trade in home-made crystal sets made up from smuggled-in wires and crystals. They were minute and the reception had a habit of fading away in the middle of a talk or play, but they were better than nothing.

One of my biggest regrets was that we didn't have the facilities to phone out on a regular basis, which meant that I was only able to telephone my parents on two occasions before they passed away. It would have been really nice to have had long conversations with my mother or father, but sadly it was not to be. Today all prisons have telephones installed and these are used with phonecards. Some prisons restrict the amount you can buy while others allow the inmates to buy as many as they can afford. They have become as much a part of prison currency as tobacco. When I was at Blundeston, which had restricted cards, I would get extras by getting other inmates to supply me on credit. Later I would have the money sent in, or paid to an address outside. There were never any problems, as my name guaranteed any credit given. In fact to show how good my name is, shortly after arriving at Maidstone I was given sixty pounds worth of cards that had been sent down on credit from a friend in Blundeston. With this system, trust has to be earned and I am proud that I have the confidence of others.

Now that we are in the EU, I would like to see Britain fall in line with the more liberal prison regimes of our European neighbours. If this happens, one important factor might be that inmates could receive much higher wages than they do at present. Wages at the moment are minimal. Yet if they were paid what their day's labour is worth it might allow them to put something aside for when they are released. At the moment an inmate might spend a year in prison and go out of the gate with the paltry sum of fifty pounds to survive on. Immediately he is in dire straits so he reoffends and is soon back inside. Also, a lot of unrest could be avoided if like Holland, Belgium and Sweden we were allowed conjugal visits, better amenities and TV in our cells. Before anyone suggests that this would make an inmate's life too soft and almost worthwhile to be locked up for, consider the crime rate in the countries I have mentioned. I have studied the figures and can assure you they are far lower than in Britain, which speaks for itself.

Strangely enough, I have observed a change for the worse in the way inmates dress over a period of eighteen years. When I was on remand in Brixton Prison during 1968, I couldn't help but notice how well dressed the remands were as they walked round and round in circles in the exercise yard. From Brixton I was moved to Parkhurst on the Isle of Wight to begin my prison sentence. I served eighteen years there until I was shifted to Wandsworth on what is called a laydown. It means you are banged up for twenty-three hours a day, seven days a week. This is a punishment without reason and even if you manage to force a reason out of the system it makes no sense and is utter rubbish. I had to put up with that for a month before being taken to spend another month on the ground-floor prison block. Pulling myself up by the bars I looked out into the yard and there were the remands – a different lot after eighteen years, but still circling around and around. Gone were the smart clothes and suits. In fact the lot of them looked like tramps with their tatty jackets and scruffy shoes. I couldn't believe how things had changed so drastically from my days when a man was proud of his appearance.

Apart from the loss of liberty, prison life can be very stressful. It increases paranoia and there can be symptoms of blushing-up and feeling uncomfortable when an inmate is suddenly confronted by another, even if they are close friends. I am not sure what causes this but have suffered this myself on occasions. Claustrophobia is something else I have been a victim of, particularly when in a cell with a group of people. It usually helps if I strip to the waist and remember to keep calm. The cause may be due to all the time I have done inside, disorientation, or the fact that we all live on top of each other on a daily basis in this strange environment. It should be remembered that one is never, I repeat never, totally relaxed in a prison regime. One is always alert and partially tense when passing anyone on the staircase, yard or field. Each prisoner will quickly glance at the other, aware that some cons carry weapons and might be potentially violent. This weighing up of every situation eventually becomes second nature, and not to see the same degree of watchfulness in others can seem strange. An example of this came to me when I was returning to Parkhurst on the ferry after having been on a visit to see my brother Ronnie. I was inside the prison van but because I needed to use the toilet I had to be escorted, in handcuffs, to the WC, situated in the bar area. I was chained to a screw and no one seemed to notice. People were passing to and fro, locked in their own thoughts, without giving me or their fellow passengers a cursory glance. To me this was totally alien, in that I noted their every movement.

My visits to Ron take place every three or four months and though the distance is shorter than it used to be the journey is no less arduous. I am taken from Maidstone to Broadmoor in a Cat. A security van and handcuffed on the two-hour journey. I am not happy with this arrangement, for I would pose no threat of escape if they allowed me the small comfort of travelling in a car, but I have no control over how I am treated. My meeting with Ron takes place in a small private room and not in the main visiting room where most of the other patients get their visits, including the Yorkshire Ripper, Peter Sutcliffe. Ronnie hates him in particular because he is a cocky, arrogant man, so he arranged to have him stabbed, which was carried out successfully when another patient plunged a pen into his eye.

I spend a lot of time in the gym but when I am in my cell my exercise is less strenuous. Nine years ago I taught myself yoga from books and papers, which I have found very beneficial for keeping me supple. The quiet exercises also give me time for contemplation in which I analyse myself. One of my conclusions is how I have changed over the years. The most obvious to me is how I do not react to slight in the same way I did years ago. There are two reasons for this. One is that if I had not trained myself to be more tolerant of others I would have constantly been in trouble, with the result that I would have ended up in Broadmoor or Rampton. The other is that I have learnt to express myself verbally. In my younger years a word in the wrong place would mean a punch in the jaw for someone and I have to admit I did get a kick out of it. But now, hating violence as I do, I prefer the more diplomatic response of talking out a problem. Apart from anything else I suppose the passing of the years has brought about a certain mellowing in my aggression.

It is difficult to reply to every letter I receive. They run into hundreds and have earned me the title of 'Censor's Nightmare'. Many are from friends, but more are from total strangers offering their support in my plight against what they see as my unfair length of sentence. These supportive letters come not only from all parts of this country, but as far away as America, South Africa and Australia. I am grateful for every one of them, but as it is physically impossible to answer all of them, I pass some on to other inmates so that they can contact the writers. It's amazing how many lonely people there are in the world today. This lends truth to the old adage that it is possible to be lonely even in a crowd. Sometimes I feel like the director of a lonely hearts' club as

I have introduced three or four pen pals who have gone on to marry each other.

Weekly visits are something I look forward to and I'm fortunate that many celebrities make the effort to come and see me. Some of them are from the world of boxing, like World Champions John H. Stracey and John Conte. Until his death a few years ago Jack 'Kid' Berg, the World Champion, often came to see me with my friend Alex Stean, the boxing promoter. Jack was a wonderful character, and would amuse us by showing his skill at removing someone's wristwatch without them knowing it.

There has always been speculation about a conflict between the Richardsons, Frankie Fraser and the Krays. But recent newspaper reports of a visit to me by Charlie and Frank have hopefully put the matter to bed. I spent one of the best visiting periods with them I can remember. The sincerity and warmth of friendship was paramount as we laughed, joked and talked of the past. These men have both got a great sense of humour and I hope I meet them again soon under better circumstances.

What of the future? I look forward to 1995 because there is a possibility that a date for my parole may be determined. On the other hand I may get a knock-back, but either way I shall approach what lies head in the same way I did in the ring all those years ago. 'Get fit, get in the ring early, and get it over with as soon as possible.' However uncertain the years ahead are I can still plan what I will do on eventual release. One of these plans will be to buy a large house in the country where any of my friends can stay if they wish to do so. Of course, that would depend on the cash situation at the time, for though it is generally thought that Ron and myself have unlimited capital, that is not the case. I won't deny that we have had considerable money in the past, but we've never been savers and right at this moment we are both broke.

I have to say I have enjoyed going through the memories of my past. It has given me a chance to visualise old friends and family and walk down roads I have been prevented from doing due to my present incarceration. It has been an emotional journey peopled as it has been by so many who are no longer with us. It has made me realise what a waste the last twenty-six years have been and the heartache it caused many, particularly my mother and father.

Last night I dreamt I was going to a drinking club. It was large and pale in colour, but before entering I paused and decided that instead I would spend the night in the company of my parents. In my mind I approached their home in Vallance Road, greatly excited to be seeing them again. Then reality caught up with me. I woke in my cell here at Maidstone feeling bitterly sad as the harsh fact swept over me, that they are no longer with me. With a heavy heart I rose in the cold light of morning, made my bed and prepared myself for yet another day behind prison walls.

Afterword

A contemporary account of Ron and Reg from an interview with John Heibner in Maidstone Prison.

I had turned twenty-one when I lived in Corfield Street, Bethnal Green, with my wife June and two small children. The twins used to live in Vallance Road two turnings away, and their Aunt May and her husband Albert lived in one of the old houses on the same road. Often I would drop in to see May and she would sit me down in the small, cosy but comfortable living room with a nice cup of tea and biscuits. She was a very down-to-earth woman and spoke her mind with abruptness, if occasion required, but she was a genuine lady and a dear friend who always took the time to stop and talk to me along the Green whenever she set eyes on me.

Tony Lambrianou lived with his wife Pat on the opposite side of Bethnal Green Road, in Blythe Street, where on the corner was Peter's Café. Tony and I were always frequenting the local pubs and clubs, standing on the corner outside Dixon's betting shop for hours chatting with local boys, or popping into the café to eat a meal – invariably on the slate. One night Tony and I were in the Queen's Arms public house in Hackney Road, when Tony suggested I went with him round to the Old Horns public house, to see the twins. He wanted to introduce me to Ronnie and Reg, who held court there most nights in case anyone should need a favour, of which there were many.

They were there most nights, but if the venue had to be changed a message was sent through the grapevine for certain people to know. Information always had a tendency to reach the twins before anyone else, including the police, so one can envisage their power. Even villains who were aware the twins were in the neighbourhood ensured they were on their best behaviour. No one relished the prospect of being sought out to attend Ronnie's displeasure and Reg's presence. But together they kept a sense of order where order was necessary. No informers and no muggings. The East End was a safe and exciting place to live.

When Tony and I walked into the Horns through the saloon bar I had the distinct feeling that all eyes were pointed in our direction. I remember Tony saying to me, 'Whatever you do, be yourself.' Everything was quiet. Then Ronnie came over from the bar and the silence broke into a lively atmosphere – people chatting, the piano sounding in the background and someone on the small stage was singing into the microphone. Ronnie had a soft smile on his face and was immaculately dressed in a finely cut suit. He extended his hand to Tony and asked, 'Who is your young friend?' Over time I noticed that Ron had a dry wit and the ability to make you laugh without your being aware of it. But this was my first meeting with Ronnie Kray and I was struck by the presence he emanated. We eventually became good friends and it was not long before he introduced me to Reg and other friends.

That first meeting remains vivid in my mind. Ronnie invited me to join him and Reg and a party of friends to a nightclub in Mayfair. As we made ready to leave the Horns I remember the coat that Ron shrugged on. It was a delicately cut, double-breasted vicuna overcoat with a half belt at the back and a small vent. On his small finger he wore a white-gold clustered ring ingrained with forty tiny diamonds, and on his wrist a thin white-gold diamond watch.

My first impression of Reg was that he reminded me of a predator. He stood off to one side of the pub with his group of friends – all formidable characters – deep in conversation, though constantly alert like a panther conscious of its surroundings. He weighed around the middleweight limit, lean, poised and ready to strike. He was the very epitome of coolness but at the same time calculating and extremely capable.

When Ronnie discovered that I used to box, straight away he wanted to see me in the ring. He contacted Tony, a dear friend of his and Reg's, who was senior coach at the Repton Boxing Club in Bethnal Green. The Repton was considered to be the best boxing club in the country as it produced several world champions in the form of John H. Stracey and Maurice Hope. Ron had Tony Burns put me in the ring with Stracey, and with Reg, and he and his entourage watched me box three rounds with him. Satisfied, he asked Tony Burns to look after me. The twins naturally kept a keen interest in the local clubs and charities.

On a later occasion, when I reached the Horns I noticed a fleet of fashionable cars parked directly outside both entrances – the most distinctive one being a large maroon Rolls-Royce saloon, which apparently belonged to the top fashion photographer David Bailey, who worked for *Vogue* at the time. As I walked through the door to the saloon bar I could see David Bailey setting up his camera and gadgets ready to take a shot. Ronnie was the centre of it all, introducing people to Bailey and Frances Wyndham. Regrettably, while I was in the lavatory Bailey gathered the twins and their friends together and took some memorable photos, which I should have been in.

Occasionally I would get a call from Ronnie inviting me to his flat in Bunhill Row. So I would walk the short distance from the Green. Braithwaite House was situated in a block raised off the ground on concrete slabs. There were two enormous lifts at ground level that would whisk you up to the ninth floor. No. 43 was the twins' residence. I rang the buzzer and could see someone coming down the stairs through the frosted glass. Carol, Reggie's girlfriend, opened the door and let me in. As one entered through the front door and stood in the tiny hallway, perhaps half a dozen thickly carpeted steps took one up to the living room directly and to the right through sliding doors was the kitchen, which looked out through picture windows upon a breathtaking sight. All the main monumental buildings of the City were visible. St Paul's Cathedral, the Bank of England, etc. Ronnie sat in a soft maroon velvet armchair in shirt sleeves rolled up to below the elbows, wearing gold-rimmed glasses, with an enormous boa constrictor wrapped around his arm. He beckoned me to stroke it, which I did very reluctantly. Against the wall to the left of where Ron sat, a tank that housed the snakes stood upon high legs. Ronnie told me they could not find the other snake and that it was probably somewhere in the drying cupboard. Reg sat on the matching coloured divan, his feet curled up, smoking a cigarette. Ron said the names of the snakes were Gerrard and Read, the names of the two detectives who arrested them for demanding money with menaces in 1964.

One weekend Ronnie decided he wanted to go to the country for a few days to the mansion he owned with Reg in a beautiful village in Suffolk. He also wanted to see his mother Violet and father Charlie who were living there at the time. With Ron, Reg, Dick Morgan, myself and Bender, who was driving, our journey through the Essex countryside was pleasant, and when we reached the village it had a quiet, peaceful appearance. The car slowed as we entered the main street, then suddenly took a sharp right-hand turn onto a gravel path which wound round to stop directly in front of a long white wooden gate, on which was emblazoned 'The Brooks'. This was the twins' mansion in Bilstone, Suffolk. Terry Bender got out of the car and opened the gate, then drove a few paces inside a curved gravel road which went round to the left, adorned on each side by expressive pointed ferns. Just inside the gate, directly on the left, stood the most exquisite pink cottage one could imagine. Inside it was small but neat and comfortable. Ronnie introduced me to his mother Violet and father Charlie Kray in the kitchen. My first impression was the humility which emanated from Violet, I couldn't help but notice the sheer delight expressed in her eyes at seeing the twins.

Ron and Reg showed me around the grounds of the mansion, which covered several acres. We followed the winding road to the main house itself, which was in the process of being renovated and awaiting the builders' touch. In the barn a long, black leather punchbag filled with sand hung from one of the beams. This was for Reggie to work out on. There was a grass tennis court, a brook running through the land, and chickens and a donkey as well as geese.

Sunday dinner was salt beef and boiled potatoes. The meal in itself was a traditional East End dinner and far too much for me to eat, though I expressed my gratitude and apologised for not being able to eat it all. In the afternoon, prior to returning to London, Ron wanted to drive over to an estate several miles away from The Brooks to see a friend. The estate was magnificent, with imposing half-moon gates opening onto a drawbridge that led across a moat into a huge medieval castle. The residence was that of Geoff Allan, a very dear friend of the twins.

One memory that springs to mind is of going to Bilstone village with Ronnie one Sunday morning. The day was brisk and Ronnie had suggested I go with him to the shop to fetch the morning papers. Before we departed on our short journey, Ronnie picked up a beautiful ornamental ebony walking stick. I think I remember him telling me this had been given to him by Billy Hill when he and Reg went out to Tangiers on an invitation. The stick was of the hardest wood and shiny, with the handle a figure in the shape of a head. Ronnie looked quite the country squire with his gold-rimmed glasses, white open-necked shirt, sleeves rolled up to below the elbows, his suit trousers with turn-ups and shiny black lace-up shoes. I can see Ronnie walking into the local shop flourishing his walking stick as though it were yesterday. The shop was small and packed and everyone looked directly at us, yet the atmosphere seemed quite relaxed as they recognised Ronnie as one of their neighbours. I can imagine they had no idea of his importance on the London scene.

*

Following this period the twins were arrested. I can recall my horror at the savage sentences they were given. Not long afterwards I would be given an equally long sentence myself for an alleged murder and be spending time with them in the same prisons.

I have a great sense of nostalgia for those days gone by. Life was fun and exciting and made much more so by being in the company of Reggie and Ronnie. They both brought the whole scene alive and their like will never be seen again.

GODFATHER
OF NIGHT

My Life in America's Hidden Greek Mafia

Kevin Pappas

Growing up in Tarpon Springs, Florida – the seaside
headquarters of the Greek mafia – Kevin Cunningham fell
in love with Greek culture and hoped to become part of it. But
when he was seventeen his world turned upside-down: from his
deathbed, the man he'd always called dad told him he
was the illegitimate son of the local crime boss.

When Kevin's attempts to gain recognition from his real father
failed, he entered into a life of crime, adopting the family name
and quickly escalating from swindling tourists to moving cocaine,
gun-running and racketeering. Having squared off against the FBI
and the DEA, and with most of his crew dead, Kevin was locked
up on two consecutive life terms. But that's only the beginning
of the story – from helping authorities capture major criminals,
outwitting the system, and ultimately finding redemption, Kevin's
story will leave true crime buffs shaking their heads.

'A powerful and honest account of how tough life can be
if you choose to live by the sword'
Sun

978-1-8474-4343-4

Other bestselling titles available by mail

☐ Godfather of Night   Kevin Pappas   £6.99

The prices shown above are correct at time of going to press. However, the publishers reserve the right to increase prices on covers from those previously advertised, without further notice.

— sphere —

Please allow for postage and packing: **Free UK delivery.**
Europe: add 25% of retail price; Rest of World: 45% of retail price.

To order any of the above or any other Sphere titles, please call our credit card orderline or fill in this coupon and send/fax it to:

Sphere, PO Box 121, Kettering, Northants NN14 4ZQ
Fax: 01832 733076   Tel: 01832 737526
Email: aspenhouse@FSBDial.co.uk

☐ I enclose a UK bank cheque made payable to Sphere for £ . .
☐ Please charge £ . . . . to my Visa/Delta/Maestro

Expiry Date [ ][ ][ ][ ]   Maestro Issue No. [ ][ ]

NAME (BLOCK LETTERS please) . . . .
ADDRESS . . . .
. . . .
. . . .
Postcode . . . . Telephone . . . .
Signature . . . .

Please allow 28 days for delivery within the UK. Offer subject to price and availability.